ALAN ALDA:
The 1983 Biography

RAYMOND STRAIT

Post Hill
PRESS

A POST HILL PRESS BOOK
ISBN: 978-1-64293-134-1

Cover art by Cody Corcoran
Interior design and layout by Sarah Heneghan

This is a work of nonfiction. All events, names, and locations are described accurately at the time of the writing of the book.

Post Hill Press
New York • Nashville
posthillpress.com

Published in the United States of America

CHAPTER 1

Alfonso Giovanni Giuseppe Roberto D'Abruzzo probably has no meaning to anyone except the man who was born with that name (or perhaps his immediate family). Take the "Al" from Alfonso, tie it to "D'A" from D'Abruzzo, put it in proper form, then add to that "Robert" from Roberto, and it becomes Robert Alda. Robert Alda, whose history to most moviegoers begins with his portrayal of George Gershwin in the 1945 Warner Brothers film *Rhapsody in Blue* and culminates in the international superstardom of his oldest son as the character of Hawkeye in television's long-running primetime sit-com "M*A*S*H."

Born in New York City on February 26, 1914, Robert's parents were Anthony and Frances (Tumillo) D'Abruzzo. He was the eldest of three children. Anthony, a barber by profession, plied his trade on steamboats operated by United Fruit Company until he realized he wasn't seeing enough of his growing family. After coming ashore for the last time, he barbered at the Shelton and Barclay hotels in New York City. He was an outgoing man who practiced the Old World custom of sitting down to the dinner table with his family for perhaps four or five hours in the evening where long discourses (often heated) about the day's events would be held. It was a family with few secrets, since all spoke their mind at these routine functions. Finally, Mr. D'Abruzzo would suggest a little music.

It was at that point all decorum was put to rest as the three youngsters sprang for their favorite musical instruments—Ann usually made it to the piano first; Vincent took over on the drums; and Robert picked up the clarinet, although he had some ability on the other two instruments. Two of the children's uncles who played in a regular orchestra would often join in with saxophone and banjo while the senior D'Abruzzo strummed away on a mandolin he brought to America with him from his native Italy. Although Mrs. D'Abruzzo was also Italian, she had been born in the United States.

From the age of five or six, young Alfonso was permitted to go into midtown Manhattan alone. It became a subject of after-dinner conversations in the family—how he guided his grandfather home from Albany by train and subway at such a tender age. He studied the maps of New York City and its suburbs and knew the subway system as well as he knew the Latin litany performed at mass every Sunday.

Graduating from Stuyvesant High School with ease at sixteen, he was then enrolled in an architectural course at New York University. His father encouraged him to "find a profession with integrity." There were nine medical men in the D'Abruzzo family: three physicians, three druggists, and an equal number of dentists. His father often pointed with pride to their accomplishments and status in the community. It was a time when to be a professional man was to be "respected."

The architectural firm of Cross and Cross was one of the finest in New York City. It was owned by two brothers who, as it happened, were shaved every morning by Mr. D'Abruzzo. It was at his father's encouragement that young Alfonso had entered the university to study architecture, because he had worked out a scheme with the Cross brothers for his son to attend school in the mornings and work for Cross and Cross in the afternoons. It was the best of lives—going to school and at the same time earning money.

In addition to his regular courses, he was taking pre- med subjects—biology, chemistry—because always in the back of his mind was the family "medical tradition." Privately, Alfonso's medical relatives all told him to forget medicine. "It's a miserable life," one said.

Another admonished him not to do it. "You're always being called out in the middle of the night to deliver babies or sit by a bedside waiting for temperatures to drop when it is ten below zero outside. It isn't worth it. People are often ungrateful after the crisis passes." That was quite true, since many times they were not paid for their services, and when they were it might be in the form of poultry or vegetables, because the patient either had no money or chose to spend it on more "tangible" items.

Alfonso saw their unified front against a medical career as an omen. He'd have to give some thought to other kinds of work.

His salary at Cross and Cross of twenty-five dollars a week wasn't bad. He was young. With no obligations and no family of his own, he was feeling "free as a breeze."

The country was also feeling a spirit of freedom and adventure. Although silent movies were still the big thing in films, Al Jolson and Warner Brothers had electrified the world with the first talking picture, *The Jazz Singer*, and Hollywood was becoming the entertainment capitol of the world. Garbo would successfully make the transition from silents to talkies, but many of the great film stars of the day would soon pass out of the picture simply because their squeaky voices did not match their glamorous images. It was the twilight of the first "jazz age" but the memory lingered on through music and the idiom of the times with such expressions as "bump off," "belly laugh," "jalopy," "screwy," and "sex appeal"—reminders of that wonderful time that is still nostalgically with us.

Marathon dancing was just coming into style, and it would not be long until poverty would become a way of life for nearly forty million Americans. New York City was not, as yet, touched by the misery soon to be felt by most of the world, and certainly a young man with nine medical men in the family had no need to worry about such things.

Haircuts could be purchased for twenty cents with a shave that included "bay rum and hot towel" for ten cents extra. "Things" were cheap. Herbert Hoover was still a very popular president who continued to promise more prosperity for the country. Franklin Delano Roosevelt, then governor of New York, was in total disagreement with Mr. Hoover politically and, in spite of being handicapped by crippling polio and confined to a wheelchair, he already had his mind and faculties at work with the intent of taking Mr. Hoover's place behind the desk of the oval office at 1600 Pennsylvania Avenue in Washington, D.C. in the next Presidential election.

But then Robert Burns' warning about "the best laid schemes of mice and men" took on a new meaning when the world turned upside down in October 1929. The stock market crashed. The show business trade magazine *Variety* chronicled it, WALL STREET LAYS AN EGG. Alfonso's employers, Cross and Cross, went down with a deafening thud, and he found himself unemployed. Not only was he left without a job, but because of his hard study and close work, his eyesight began to fade. "When I first went to work, I had perfect vision," he remembers, "but inside of a year I was wearing glasses. By 1932, when the bottom fell out of everything, I was wearing lenses as thick as a T-bone steak."

He never abandoned his dream (although he did not discuss it in front of his father, who had little regard for show business) of being an actor. Out of work with little prospect of any future employment, he jumped at the opportunity to enter an amateur contest as a singer. It was no ordinary amateur hour. The Manhattan Academy of Music was offering a twenty-five-dollar first prize for the entrant who could best sing the title song of a new movie starring Charles Farrell and Janet Gaynor (who became America's darlings in *Seventh Heaven*) called *Merely Mary Ann*. Alda won hands down and received the first-prize money, which was as much as he made for a full week's work at Cross and Cross. He was ecstatic. It became obvious to him that if he could make that kind of money for ten minutes of pleasure, then he was in the wrong business all along and should seek a career in show business. He recently boasted, "That was my last performance as an amateur," although in early interviews before he became a star, he revealed that he sang for several years after the contest, "always as an amateur, at contests, dances, and weddings." When not singing, he worked as a clerk in a department store, as a singing usher at the Orpheum Theater on Eighty-sixth Street, and at various other jobs. It was during the depression and he, like other young men, took whatever was available.

While working at the Orpheum, he met a young man—also a singing usher—who lived in the building next door to Alda, as they discovered while walking home from the subway after work one night. By this time, he had dropped "Alfonso" and had adopted the short form of Robert— Bob. Frank Brown, his co-worker and next-door neighbor would leave him sometime after midnight, entering his own building, with "Good night, Bob. I better get inside and eat the bedtime snack my sister leaves for me."

One evening as Alda entered the neighborhood delicatessen his mind was on something else, and he bumped into someone loaded down with packages. The collision ended up with packages scattered about on the sidewalk and the other person looking somewhere between puzzled and disgusted. It turned out to be Frank's sister Joan, who, according to Bob Alda, "was blonde and lovely and the most beautiful creature I'd ever seen." Unaware that she was Frank's sister and living next door to him all this time, he asked the delicatessen owner who she was.

He learned that her name was Joan Brown, a beauty contest winner who had recently returned from a year's tour with Franchon and Marco's *Venuses of 1930*. A former Miss Manhattan, she appeared bound for a career in show business as a dancer and perhaps an actress. Fate intervened, however, and her show business career changed course. After a year of meeting over ham on rye and "large hunks of cheesecake" and taking long walks around Gramercy Park, they married. Some reports say their nuptials took place in September 1932, others indicate New Year's Eve of that same year. Nonetheless, it was a big wedding with "dozens of guests."

Now married with responsibilities, Bob Alda had to work all the harder to make ends meet. He was still moving from one job to another with a degree of regularity. Because of the amateur contest he had won, he was given a fifteen-minute sustaining program as a singer over WOV radio on Thirty-seventh Street. He maneuvered his lunch hour at B. Altman's department store so that he could keep the radio job. Although he was not replacing Russ Columbo or Bing Crosby in the baritone department, he did manage to have his picture in the window of a local five-and-dime store.

He was not interested in department-store work. What held his interest at B. Altman's was the weekly salary, which helped him and his new wife survive. Altman's settled his quandary. One day he was fired during a mass layoff caused by the depression. He was now free to offer himself totally to show business on a full-time basis. Except for his nonpaying radio stint (which he considered "good exposure"), there was no immediate work. His big show-business "break" came when he was hired as an usher at the Palace Theater. Although the wages were skimpy, he saw it as a great opportunity.

"The film playing was Frank Buck's *Bring 'Em Back Alive*. I remember it vividly," he recalls. "It was so popular that people stood in line for hours to see it. Since we had no reserved seats and there were always more patrons than space in which to seat them, it was common practice for moviegoers to slip the usher a tip for assurance that they would be seated." Alda often would pick up an easy twenty-five dollars extra on weekends.

There is some confusion about when the following took place. Some say it was during his first stint as a singing usher, but later interviews with Alda alter that somewhat. In any event, the following account is worth repeating because the sequence of events isn't as important as how it came about. Alda claims that when the Frank Buck film closed, he got a job with another theater uptown. It was indeed the time of "amateur contests" because there was so much unemployment that young hopefuls would take a shot at anything in order to pick up some extra cash. Alda, with a fair baritone voice and no lack of confidence in his own ability, cooked up a scheme to further his ambitions: "I tipped the master of ceremonies to put me on as 'The Singing Usher.' I was given a nice buildup by the emcee, who asked the audience to 'give one of our own gang a chance.'" Alda bounced out on the stage filled with enthusiasm, winked at the audience, and burst into "The Man on the Flying Trapeze," one of the hit songs of the day. He believes his usher's suit helped him more than the Master of Ceremonies' efforts. He was given a resounding reception by the audience, and a savvy theater manager hired him as a regular attraction.

He was an attraction that did seem to bring in more people to the theater, which did not make the manager of a rival theater across the street happy. Never one to pass up a good thing, the other theater manager lured Alda into his theater for ten dollars a week more than he was making (which was five dollars). Alda admits, "I wasn't very loyal. All the guy had to do was make me an offer." Although he was "working around," his ambition was elsewhere. "I looked toward burlesque, rather than wait around for my big break on Broadway." He was a young man in a hurry. Joan, apparently abandoning whatever ambitions she had in show business, went along with Bob's theatrical aspirations and was content to be a wife and later a devoted mother.

Alda was really lucky to be working at all. The financial slump and unemployment that began with the stock market crash in 1929 was nearing a peak, and New York's streets were filled with former financial giants selling apples on street corners. Many, unable to handle their fall from power and wealth, committed suicide by jumping out of windows or putting guns to their temples. Prohibition was on and, because it was illegal to sell alcohol for any purpose other than medicinal, racketeers like Al Capone in Chicago were able to clean up with bootleg booze and speakeasies, often slaughtering one another in the streets during fights over territorial jurisdictions. President Roosevelt's "New Deal" programs were the law of the land and Americans took hope in his message that all the country need fear was "fear itself." But although he had swung into office dramatically with a theme song that said, "Happy Days Are Here Again," happy days for the nation as a whole were a long way off.

The handsome young Alda was undaunted by national gloom or unstable economic news. He pursued his newfound career with great diligence and determination, taking whatever problems he and his wife might have to mass on Sunday mornings and leaving them there. Like his parents, he was a devout Catholic with deep religious convictions.

Singing in a radio station was nice, but it was not enough. Alda's ambition was insatiable. He wanted to sing before a theater audience—the big time. It was certainly no surprise to those who knew him when he abandoned radio and went into burlesque as a "straight man" to comics. This move gave him the opportunity not only to continue singing but to test his mettle in comedy and see if he had the dramatic ability to deliver lines effectively. Of course, he did. During the next few years, he was a voracious student of anything and everything in the entertainment world. It was about this same time that Joan broke the news that he should start thinking about his heir apparent, who was due to arrive sometime during the coming winter.

Although burlesque was generally considered the sleazier side of show business, Alda defended it with pointed conviction. "No matter what anybody says," he declared, "burlesque is full of the hardest-working, most serious-minded people in the world. All burlesque actors want to buy a farm and retire—and me, too!" An old adage in burlesque is that, "There is nothing that can't be done." Bob Alda subscribed to that philosophy. During a five-year stint with Minsky's, he did everything and never complained. "The work has always been steady and the pay good," he said. "I owe burlesque a lot." Perhaps he did, but he certainly earned his keep. He played everything from juveniles to drunks, dopes to derelicts. As often as fifty or sixty times a day, he had to make his voice heard over the blare of the orchestra, its trumpets screaming, and endure the heavy cigar smoke that often created a curtain between him and the audience, hovering like a dark cloud over the orchestra pit. Not only did he play straight men for the comics, but he also filled in as a comic if a comic got sick. Sometimes he sold chocolate bars between acts—money was money, no matter how it was earned. In retrospect, he says of burlesque, "I looked upon it as an education. It taught me a lot of things—and built me a swell bank account."

Burlesque gave him the opportunity to work with and observe the greats of the burlesque stage both on Broadway and at the resort watering holes in the Catskill Mountains, better known as the "Borscht Circuit." There, he met and shared the stage with the likes of Rags Ragsland, Bud Abbott, and Phil Silvers. One burlesque critic of the time credited Alda with "uncorking a good voice."

On January 28, 1936—a cold blustery day in New York—Joan Alda went into labor. After many hours, an exhausted Joan Alda finally gave birth to a son (their only child), who was given the shortened name of Alan (from Alfonso) and immediately became known to one and all as "Allie," a name that sticks with him even today.

Barely twenty-one years old himself, Alda had very little to offer his new son other than love and a roof over his head. He continued to work in the Catskills and around New York City, but nothing sensational was happening, although he never missed a chance to better himself. He wanted more than burlesque. During the summertime when work was slow, he would play in stock—which was becoming more important on the Borscht Circuit. Looking toward Broadway, he talked with agents and pitched his best side, hoping for an opportunity to do a big Broadway production.

On one occasion, Hollywood producer Jesse L. Lasky was conducting his talent show, called "Gateway to Hollywood," on the radio. Bob Alda sent in a photograph of himself along with a "brilliant" bio. Both the photo and bio were returned with the form-letter rejection of "Don't call us, we'll call you." It was an incident that would give Alda a chance to needle Lasky in the years to come, because Lasky was to produce the George Gershwin story that made Alda a movie star.

In 1937, he had the distinction of being one of the first performers on television. The medium would not be formally introduced to the world until the 1939 New York World's Fair, but a variety program called "Alda and Henry," which teamed Bob and Hank Henry, was shown over CBS. The only viewers (outside the studio) were travelers who surrounded a primitive television set located in Grand Central Station. It was a curiosity. Viewers said, "Well, I'll be damned" and quickly rushed away to catch their commuter trains, forgetting all about television. It was, to most, just another of those electrical fads that they'd probably never hear of again.

Alda was tiring of burlesque, although he and Henry were popular—just as Abbott and Costello had been earlier. Bob and Hank often did the same routines as Abbott and Costello. Alda likes to tell about a luncheon for exhibitors at Warner Brothers some years later when he was a contract player there. "Bud Abbott was suddenly taken ill and I stepped in without a rehearsal and did the 'baseball' routine with Lou Costello—without a rehearsal. It was one of my favorite skits and I knew it well." He remembers that Jack Warner thought it was too "lowbrow" for a man who was playing the immortal George Gershwin. Alda, he opined, should be above such nonsense.

Alan Alda became his father's shadow, watching everything his father did and enjoying it. Alda and Henry worked together until 1941. Shortly after the Japanese assault on Pearl Harbor and America's official entry into World War II, Hank Henry was drafted into the army and Bob Alda became a solo act—almost. From time to time, young Alan would be brought onstage in some bit of comedic nonsense that was sure to guarantee a sympathetic audience and an extra laugh. Alda senior remembers the first time he brought Alan onto a stage during his early appearances in the Catskills: "He was six months old and I was working in a show with Joey Adams. It was at one of the resort hotels. We brought Alan onstage in his high chair, and of course the audience loved it. It was during the time when Major Bowes had his famous amateur hour on radio and the gong he would hit to remove a contestant who wasn't cutting it (a gong that was almost as famous as the major himself). There was a little bell on Alan's high chair. He sat there and watched the act with devoted interest until we got to the finale—which was reserved, of course, for Joey Adams' big number. Alan picked that particular moment to start ringing the bell on his high chair (a la Major Bowes) for all he was worth. Of course, the audience roared and he totally upstaged Joey Adams." It was

Alan Alda's first stage appearance, and the warm reception he received encouraged his father to bring him into the act often.

It was the beginning of a romance with acting that has been with Alan Alda throughout his life, at times resembling a love/hate relationship that we will see develop over the years as his story unfolds.

When he was no more than three years old, he played games with stagehands and performers behind the curtains while his father MC'd the shows before the footlights. The theater became a second home for him, and he was a quick study, as they say in show business. He absorbed theatrical lingo and habits like a sponge. He also learned that he liked girls, even if they were light-years older than he. Alan saw it as a "wonderful place to learn about the theater," an atmosphere in which he could see "both the trick and how the magician performs it." He loved chorus girls and they made a big fuss over him. Dancers and strippers became his friends and were far more exciting than anyone else he met. "Even though I was only three years old, I appreciated femininity. It was exciting to me. Maybe adults don't know it, but kids have sexual feelings—an awareness of sex—even at such an early age. I became their dressing-room mascot."

The strippers found Alan as entertaining as he did them. If they were changing clothes and asked him to turn his head, he obliged. Little did they suspect that he immediately buried his head in their soft and feminine-smelling costumes. He admits to having been "more turned on by their perfumed garments than by all the nakedness behind me." To him they were as warm and lovely as the silken negligees tossed carelessly across the back of a chair in the dressing room.

Joan Alda never tried to be a part of the spotlight. She preferred always to be in the background, allowing the men in her life to take the forefront. Talking with people who knew the Aldas during that time, they saw Joan Alda without exception as "a quiet, shy but fun person to be with who allowed Robert great latitude with the upbringing of Allie." Alan remembers as one of his fondest memories "walking down Broadway or through Central Park with my father's hand clasped in mine close to my face." Mrs. Alda seems to have understood the traditional Old World Italian custom of men having the voice and women being supportive. She was always considered the perfect wife for Robert and a mother without peer. Some family friends say that although Alan seemed, from a very early age, to want to follow in his father's footsteps, his personality and mannerisms are those of his mother.

In early 1942, Robert Alda made a cross-country, six-month USO national tour with the "Fun for Your Money" unit—playing 125 army and navy bases from coast to coast. Ever the man of all seasons in the theater, Robert acted as MC, did leads in dramatic skits, played straight man for the comics, and even joined the chorus as a dancer. It was difficult work, but his experience in burlesque had prepped him for the grueling tour and he fared well.

Led by stars like Tyrone Power, Clark Gable, and Jimmy Stewart, many of the major male screen stars were either being drafted or volunteering for military service. Hollywood movie moguls and studio executives went head-hunting for talent wherever it could be found—and it could be found in New York both on and off Broadway. It was practically predestined that a man with Alda's romantic looks would be tabbed by one of the motion-picture studios. Talent was not necessarily a prerequisite. Hollywood was overrun with drama coaches and every studio had its own coaching staff. Alda, however, had both looks and talent.

Back from his lengthy tour, Alda checked in with his agent, who sent him to see Steve Trilling, Jack Warner's assistant, who was in New York representing Warner Brothers in their quest for new faces—especially one "with the Gershwin quality." Jack Warner said, "I don't give a damn about long careers. We need faces to fill in until our stars come home from the war." Trilling covered Broadway and the Catskills and was able to sign a few actors for his studio. When he returned to Hollywood, however, there was one actor he strongly recommended to his boss—a Cary Grant type named Robert Alda. He was so persuasive that Jack Warner agreed to bring Alda to Hollywood and give him a screen test with a contract possibly in the offing. One test was not enough. It was followed by numerous others, which kept Alda in Hollywood for seven weeks, all expenses paid.

It was only after Trilling returned from New York that Alda received any positive word as to his future. One night Trilling called him and said, "Relax, Bob. You now have a long-term contract with Warner Brothers." Even with a contract, he had no idea what Jack Warner had in mind for him at the big studio. Once the deal was set, Alda underwent even more testing without knowing what the tests were for. The Gershwin project was very hush-hush. It is believed that Jack Warner was afraid MGM and Louis B. Mayer would steal the idea and make the Gershwin story into a picture before the Warner Brothers film could get off the ground. But the studio executives were finally convinced that Robert Alda could handle the role of George Gershwin in *Rhapsody in Blue*. Alda gives John Garfield, another Warner's contract star, credit for bringing his name to the attention of the studio brass. "Fate and circumstance play an important part in being successful, and don't let anybody tell you anything different," Alda says. "While I was being readied for my screen test, Garfield, who had seen me in stock back east, told the studio brass glowing stories about my ability and they took a more serious look at me."

The irony of this did not get by one producer. Shortly after it was announced that Alda would be awarded the prize role, he was sitting with Garfield and Cary Grant, having just met the two men. It was a well-publicized secret that both actors had actively sought the part—especially John Garfield. "Just think," said the producer seated with the three men, "here are two men who wanted to play George Gershwin in the same company of the man who *will* play Gershwin."

Still sharp from his burlesque routines (having never been at a loss for words), Alda quipped, "If you play your cards right, fellows, one of you may someday get a chance to play the life of Robert Alda."

There were genuine reasons why a newcomer was chosen for the part (which was highly fictionalized anyway). Primarily, it was thought that a new face who could become an instant star (a big plus for Warner's) would not outshine the Gershwin character.

Even before receiving the assignment, Alda was already on the lot doing all the things new contract players were expected to do in those days: drama lessons, singing lessons, dancing lessons. It was a routine that could be found at every major studio in the business. Actually, he did not find out about the Gershwin role until one week before principal photography (photography and shooting that involved the star) was to begin. All the other parts had already been cast.

When the Aldas moved to California with their six-year-old son, they settled into a nice cottage commensurate with Bob's income. Alan remembers it as "an ugly little shack in Hollywood." Nobody else seems to remember it as being ugly, but it was small and Joan was quite successful in her effort to give the house the warm glow of home. She was very handy and innovative at decorating on a small budget. With Bob so busy at the studio, this was a period of time in which Alan spent most of his waking hours at home with Joan rather than with his father, although they continued to be very close and even worked on comedy routines together. The Aldas were written about as "one of the happiest families in the film colony."

When the news broke that Bob Alda had been selected for one of the biggest roles of the year—that of Gershwin in *Rhapsody in Blue*—it was tantamount to announcing his stardom before one frame of film had been shot. Fan magazines converged on Alda for interviews as did Louella Parsons and Hedda Hopper, the ruling queens of Hollywood gossip. Some predicted his handsome face and masculine physique would carry him to heights heretofore attained only by superstars like Gary Cooper and Clark Gable. It was all premature Hollywood hype. Jack Warner was aware of that and thought only of how much the publicity would help make *Rhapsody in Blue* pay off big at the box office.

When production began in July of 1943, Bob Alda was riding too high on his own personal stardom to expect anything other than happy times ahead for himself, Joan, and young Allie. He obviously believed his own publicity, which was strictly "rave." He had no way of knowing that disaster lay just ahead.

CHAPTER 2

Warner Brothers Studios surrounded its newcomer with tried and proved talent. Oscar Levant, one of the great pianist interpreters of Gershwin and also a close personal friend of the composer, had one of the strongest supporting roles. Levant had a rather psychotic sense of humor that was very popular with the movie-going public. More important, he lent authenticity to the script. Joan Leslie was given the female lead and even Paul Whiteman (also close to Gershwin) and his great orchestra were cast in the film. The music was outstanding and that's about all the critics allowed the film. Unfortunately, for Alda, the picture was shelved by Warner Brothers. Jack Warner, totally disappointed in the effort, seems never to have forgiven Alda (who was no more at fault than anyone else), and as the star of the picture he bore the brunt of Warner's feelings. It would be two years before the film would be released.

In some quarters of Hollywood, Alda was gaining a reputation for being "stuck on himself." This phrase could have been applied to any number of stars. However, since he had such a publicity buildup, his opinions about himself were blown up in the grand Hollywood tradition. He told one writer that "As long as they're going to call me a star, then I'm going to live like one." The first visible sign of his taking stardom seriously was to go out and buy an eleven-acre ranch/estate in La Tuna Canyon, situated far from the Hollywood colony in the mountains on the northern perimeter of the San Fernando Valley. The place was reputed to be valued at sixty thousand dollars, so the twenty-five-thousand-dollar purchase price was a tribute to Bob's financial acumen. He boasted that the "estate" even had its own fenced mountain. Of course, the "gone Hollywood" label was again applied to the handsome young star.

Alda laughed. "Hollywood had nothing to do with it. This place was purchased with *Minsky* money."

In all fairness, there was a more important reason for buying such a large place than just having a big head. About halfway through the filming of *Rhapsody in Blue*, events took a sudden tragic turn for the Aldas. With Bob's newfound success and fame came all the trappings: the new house and a new school (private, of course) for young Allie. Joan and Bob, after looking over many brochures from private schools, decided on a popular military academy where many stars were sending their offspring. Allie had been enrolled in the new school for two weeks when he suddenly became ill. He was seven years old.

He didn't go to school one day because he wasn't feeling well. Joan sensed it was something serious. By afternoon, he was miserable and had a temperature. Bob thought it was probably just a cold or sore throat. By evening, the temperature was still rising and other symptoms manifested themselves. It was not unusual for Allie to be alone and quiet for long periods of time—but this was different. He eventually began throwing up and complained of a violent headache. Soon afterward he lost his equilibrium. Joan put him to bed with the usual nostrums of aspirin, liquids, and warm blankets. By the following morning, his body had stiffened and he was unable to tilt his head in order to drink a glass of juice.

His father still thought it was only a cold and would go away. "You know how kids are with these things," he said to Joan. "He'll be up and wanting to go outside before the day is over."

His mother didn't think so; she insisted on calling a doctor. The doctor arrived and within half an hour after his arrival, Alan was hospitalized. The diagnosis, as Joan had privately suspected all along, was polio. If she had waited, as her husband suggested, before calling in a doctor, Alan believes, "I would have been crippled and probably would never have walked again. I owe my life to my mother and her decision to get help immediately."

At that time the fatality rate for polio was extremely high, and rarely, if ever, did anyone survive without spending the rest of his life in a wheelchair or in painful braces.

For thirty years, Australian nurse Sister Elizabeth Kenny ("Sister" is the title given head nurses in the British Empire) had been practicing an unorthodox treatment for infantile paralysis (polio). Sister Kenny nursed the bush country of Australia, and many of her ministrations were of the old-fashioned commonsense variety that were not found in the stuffy medical books in Melbourne or any other major city in Australia. The accepted method of treatment for polio prior to the forties was to keep the arms and legs of the patient in tight, uncomfortable splints, rendering the limbs motionless for several months—which almost invariably did as much damage as the disease itself.

Sister Kenny had grown up on a farm in the lonely backlands, her father and mother having been Scotch-Irish pioneer settlers in southeastern Queensland, where few doctors were ever seen. Midwives and practitioners with hand-me-down knowledge took care of most medical problems. The local postmaster sometimes performed emergency surgery with his pocketknife with only a hardworking band of two-fisted women called the "bush nurses." The nurses were often alone and as Sister Kenny said, "We often had to use our own discretion." Bad roads and long distances between farms often put that discretion to the test. It was not unusual for directions for surgery to be given by telegraph—when the lines weren't down or so filled with static that it was impossible to receive messages.

While nursing in the small settlement of Pilton Hills in 1910, young Sister Kenny came upon a youngster desperately ill with symptoms totally alien to anything she'd ever encountered before. She sent a message to the nearest doctor, who lived in the village of Toowoomba, a distance of nearly fifty miles. He wired back: "Symptoms you describe clearly indicate infantile paralysis." He gave no instructions as to the prescribed treatment. He merely told her to, "Use your best observation and judgment." It did not take long for the disease to become epidemic. She hadn't been told and didn't know that the muscles were thought to be slack and sagging, that the affected parts should be immobilized by placing them in rigid casts or splints in order to prevent the strong muscles from pulling the weakened ones out of place—creating crippling deformities.

Feeling inadequate and certain she would be unable to treat the disease, she opted for treating "the symptoms" in order to ease the muscle spasms that apparently caused great pain to the patient. She applied water, heat, and blankets to the afflicted areas. Her system of care seemed to bring about a response, and soon her charges were up and about, contrary to any results ever received by the medical men. A year later, she traveled on leave to Toowoomba, where she visited with Dr. McDonnell, who had given her such sketchy advice by wire. He was, of course, doubtful of her findings and the story she told him of having "cured" the children without deformity.

The incredulous doctor said, "I want you to take one of my own cases of poliomyelitis and see what you can do with it." Undaunted and brave, perhaps because of her youth, Sister Kenny went to work. Dr. McDonnell later described his amazement at her methods: "Sister Kenny gently stripped the splints and bandages from the child's pale and aching limbs. Then she called for boiling water and a heavy blanket, and went to work. She tore the blanket into sections, which she wrung out in hot water and placed around the aching limbs. As fast as these hot packs cooled, she replaced them." In a few days she began manipulating the arms and legs of the child and started to massage the muscles. "She soon encouraged the young lad to try to move his limbs—and he did. Within weeks, the boy romped about as sturdy as ever before."

But men controlled medicine, not women, and it was not until 1933 that Sister Kenny was permitted to set up a clinic in the small village of Townsville—and only then because the treatment was very inexpensive and required more elbow grease than medicine. In spite of that, the learned conservative Australian physicians clashed with her on her methods. A royal commission was granted to the medical men so they might compare her method with the customary one. Three years later they delivered a three-hundred-page report denouncing her treatment, although it was the only known treatment that was successful.

In 1940, Dr. Wallace H. Cole, professor of orthopedic medicine, and Dr. Miland E. Knapp, professor of physical therapy (both at the University of Minnesota), invited Sister Kenny to bring her treatment to the United States. The following year, the American findings of her treatment were published in the prestigious *Journal of the American Medical Association*, the house organ of the AMA. It had been a long time, but at last Sister Elizabeth Kenny's precious and effective treatment for polio was receiving recognition. Clinics were immediately set up in certain cities in the United States and Canada where she personally trained nurses and therapists (as well as doctors) in the Kenny method. By 1942, just one year before Alan Alda was stricken with the dread disease, this country gave full recognition to Sister Kenny, and her treatment became the norm for treating polio. Still, for over thirty years, medical men around the world found excuses to prevent her discovery from legitimate medical practice. It was thought by medical experts (after Sister Kenny's treatment was accepted) that had President Roosevelt received the benefits of the Kenny treatment he might have had a total recovery from polio in its early stages.

Joan Alda was not a skeptic. She was a mother concerned about the full recovery of her young son and immediately set about to implement the Kenny method on Alan. He remembered his mother's total devotion to his illness and the cure: "There she was, every hour for months, dropping hot packs on my back and legs. I was in terrible pain all the time for the better part of a year—from the treatment, not the disease. It was a very painful process. You cut woolen blankets into squares and you fold them into triangles like large diapers, and then you boil them until they're so stinging hot the person who applies them can't even hang on to them. I remember them being dropped on me. And then they're wrapped tightly around every muscle and pinned on. Every hour. Can you imagine how hard that was? I can still smell the wool. But I think it was even harder on my parents than on me. I just felt the physical pain. They had to hear this kid they loved screaming. They had to make their kid hurt like that on an hourly basis."

Alan also recalls that "My mother was very very warm, very affectionate." It was during those months while Joan unselfishly devoted her every waking hour to Allie that the seeds of feminism took root in his fertile young mind. He says, "I didn't become a feminist because it was 'this year's cause.' I became one because of the incredible waste of half the talent in the world. The chauvinistic treatment by men in the medical profession of Sister Kenny showed me that sexism was not merely impolite—it could be lethal."

It was certainly a plus in Alda's life that his father had the means and wherewithal to provide his son with the environment that made his convalescence more bearable. The family's new estate featured an enormous swimming pool, which Alan, once he was out of bed, swam in every single day in order to strengthen the muscles that had been weakened by polio. The Alda homestead was truly a farm in the hills. It boasted stables with horses, chickens, goats, rabbits, large garage, playhouse, a main house with ten rooms plus a five-room guest cottage. Allie was never without company. Bob and Joan brought with them the habits of his family in New York. The place was usually overrun with relatives and their children. There was also an unusual houseguest. When Bob purchased the estate, he allowed an interesting clause to be part of the sales contract. "The former owner wanted to live in the guest cottage for a year, and I agreed."

It was an agreement he would later regret having made. Within a short period of time, the two stopped speaking to each other. Somehow the former owner got the idea in his head that the Aldas were planning to give up the house, so every time a tree or plant was pruned the old fellow would become hysterical. Alda was relieved when the year ended and his strange guest evacuated his digs.

The Aldas, particularly Joan, claimed to like the isolation offered by their new country home. In those days, La Tuna Canyon was far from the hustle and bustle of Hollywood. In the pine-scented mountain air, there was little thought of smog or industrial pollutants that were growing in the Los Angeles basin as a result of defense plants and attendant industries brought to a peak because of World War II. Joan loved to write poetry and the setting was perfect for that endeavor. Alan Alda's wife is also quite a prolific poet.

Alda had more in mind than merely owning a large estate. It was his plan to become a gentleman farmer and allow the place to help pay for itself. Consequently, he grew and sold a variety of fruits from the trees that abounded the acreage, plus olives and all sorts of vegetables. Labor—especially farm labor—was hard to come by during the war, so it was not unusual for the Aldas to spend time in the fields themselves. At one point Bob Alda became so involved in farming he was reported to have actually turned down some acting roles and was quoted by the Warner Brothers publicity department as saying, "One more year of farming on the Warner payroll, and I can afford to go back to my chosen profession."

As an only child, Alan was never without love and devotion, not only from his parents, but from both their families. He was doted on and given almost anything that money could buy. One of these gifts was a rifle, which, due to an unpleasant incident, nurtured the pacifism in his soul that remains in full bloom today. Among the many animals on the ranch, Alan had pet rabbits. When their ears became infected, he was introduced to an unpleasant fact of nature—the pets would have to be destroyed. He had never made a kill as a hunter, so rather than send them off to the veterinarian to be dispatched by medical euthanasia, he decided to end their existence with some target practice. The results were disastrous. He later explained his feelings to a reporter while promoting the motion picture *The Four Seasons*. "The rabbits would flop in the air and I would have to shoot them again to put them out of their pain. I started it with a feeling of exhilaration and ended it sobbing. I touched something way out of my control. I think I saw what it was like to be a sniper or a killer." The experience soured him on guns and their causes and effects forever.

If that kind of reality was painful, other experiences were not. When he was eight or nine years old, he became suspicious about just who Santa Claus was. "I wondered how, with everything Santa had to do, he could find time to trim our tree." He hid and watched while Joan, Bob, and a male friend dressed in a Santa costume proceeded to trim the family Christmas tree. Why the friend donned the Santa suit was never explained, but young and curious Allie's belief in the bearded gentleman of Christmas came to an abrupt end when one of his parents slipped and called the friend by his real name.

During the two-year period in which he was receiving daily (almost hourly) treatment for the lingering effects of his polio, Alan was tutored in academics. From all reports he was never a great student, preferring almost from the beginning to live in a world of theatrical fantasies. He was comfortable with show people and much preferred practicing Abbott and Costello routines with his father to poring over math and science books. Although the senior Alda did nothing to discourage his young son's interest in comedy or the entertainment industry, he had a secret wish that Alan would go for the medical career that he had passed over to become an actor and movie star. Nonetheless, he did not press, remembering the feelings he'd nurtured because some in his family had encouraged a medical degree when he really wanted to dance and sing. Thus it became somewhat commonplace for the two Aldas, father and son, to appear at functions around Hollywood doing comedy routines together. Their favorite, and one they gained some minor notoriety for, was a takeoff on the classic Abbott and Costello's "Who's On First." For Alan, it was great fun. For his father, it was a chance to spend more time with the youngster who brightened his life beyond all else.

During Alan's long convalescence from polio, he was given therapy, swam, and had a private tutor. Always somewhat shy, he appears to have welcomed the chance to study at home and avoid daily competition with other boys his age. A friend of his mother's says, "I've known the family for many years and I believe it was during those two years at home that he began to identify more with his mother than with his father. As he grows older, I see him more and more like her than Bob."

His return to a regular classroom was less than auspicious. If ever a child had inner conflicts, Alan Alda appears to have had a larger-than-life dose of them during his junior high school years. Leaving the comfort of the nest, where Joan gave supplication to his every wish, need, and desire, and having to fend once again for himself among his peers was more than a little traumatic. He had all the trappings of a "mama's boy," and the other boys never let him forget it for one moment. He was the constant butt of jokes, taunts, and no little amount of ridicule. For two years, he had been able to study at his own pace, be his own person without any regimentation or firm structure in his life. His parents had been ecstatic that their only child could walk, run, and function like other normal children, so there was a lot of love and very little organization in his life when he returned to school.

He has many times since confirmed that he felt like an outsider among people who were somewhat alien to his way of being.

Catholic schools can be and often are harsh in their approach to teaching. Youngsters are supposed to attend mass daily, have great respect for God, and show tremendous humility and awe for their instructors; as for young men, they are expected to be macho in the sense that tears are a sign of weakness and not participating in athletics is akin to ungodliness. That is the more or less official position—or certainly was during Alan's school years. In the locker rooms and boys' toilets it was even worse. All that pent-up religious atmosphere came apart and the weak or lame fared poorly. Older, bigger, and stronger boys went through the pecking order. Alan, never a fighter, endured the indignities perpetrated upon him. His school days at Saint Robert Bellarmine are not among his fondest memories.

Nonetheless, he did make friends—always of his own choosing—and was very popular in spite of his difficulties. He was turning the corner from puberty to adolescence. Before long his life would take on some dramatic changes, not only in physical and emotional growth, but in relocating from the West Coast to the East. It would be only the beginning of a long history of movement back and forth across the country as he matured as a man and pursued his career.

CHAPTER 3

By the age of thirteen, the once pudgy little boy had begun to grow tall and thinner. He wore hideous braces, which were the scourge of any young man of his day.

When Alan was ten or eleven, he met the young girl who would become the object of his first puppy-love affair, an affair that would endure for more than two years. Even at that early age he took the ladies more seriously than his contemporaries. Antoinette Dell'Olio's father owned show horses, which he bought or bred himself. He had purchased champion horses from movie stars, including one from cowboy and western star Gene Autry. Because of his equestrian activities, Mr. Dell'Olio met and associated with many famous stars of the day and was a good friend of both Bud Abbott and Lou Costello. Antoinette met young Allie through a rather circuitous route. Her mother and father were often guests at the home of Lou Costello and his wife, Ann. At one such social event, they met Bob and Joan Alda. Alan's father was being groomed for stardom at Warner Brothers and when he met the Italian-born Dell'Olio they became instant friends.

When the handsome young Italo-American brought his wife, Joan, and his young son Allie to visit the Dell'Olio's, the two youngsters met for the first time. "I remember how handsome Robert Alda was. He was dazzling to my pubescent little heart and his wife Joan was the most beautiful woman I had ever seen in person. Their son Allie was at a chubby stage and was wearing braces. The first time we visited, I found him very shy. But it turned out that his closest pals were his Aunt Jane, only one year older than he, and her friend Leila. Jane and Leila both attended Villa Cabrini Academy in Burbank, where I was a boarding student. Jane, who had never spoken to me before, came up to me the Monday after I met Allie and presented me with a note from him. Our "relationship" began. As Jane and Leila were day students, they arranged for Alan to come over and play ball with us after school. However, the rules were so strict for boarders like me that I had to stand inside the wall and catch the ball when Alan, with Jane and Leila, the two matchmakers, coaching, threw the ball over the wall to me."

Toni remembers that, "Jane was a lovely, pale girl, a tap dancer with long dark hair to her waist. She wore braces, just as Alan did." Jane was not the only member of Joan's family who was around a lot. "When the Aldas came to our house to visit, they always brought along members of Joan's family. I remember Agnes, Joan's mother, quite well. She really ruled the roost in her household. Her husband was a very quiet man who had very little to say. But Agnes was always very kindly toward me. I was a boarding student, while Alan was a day student, and Agnes thought it was terrible that my parents sent me to a boarding school and admonished my mother about that. 'How could you possibly send the child to live away from home?' she would ask. She was a very family-oriented lady, just as the entire Alda family—on both sides—seemed to be."

Toni had a younger sister, Anselma (shortened to Selma), who enjoyed tagging along with Alan and Toni when they went to a movie. One particular incident stands out in Toni's mind as she recalls what was also her first adventure in romance: "Alan was picking me up to see a movie and my sister was about five years old at the time and insisted on coming along. In the darkened movie house, Alan very bravely put his arm around my shoulder with his fingers dangling against Selma's shoulder where she sat next to me on the other side. I was never so embarrassed in my life when Selma, during a very hushed scene on the silver screen, blurted out in a very loud voice, 'Alan stop it!' I wanted to crawl under the seat and disappear."

"Allie, always the proper gentleman but always kidding, joking, doing impromptu skits, scared my sister silly with a rubber hand from his father's film, *The Beast with Five Fingers*." Yet he was a very attentive beau and always attended the bazaars and school functions at Villa Cabrini Academy. "He always played jokes and sight gags," she says. "He seemed to care genuinely for others." In that respect, his image over the years has remained pretty much the same. He also loved to wisecrack. Toni recalls that his two favorite expressions were "Your father's moustache," and "Antoinette, the gun moll."

His thirteenth birthday party was a big event and really climaxed the great romance between him and Toni. She remembers: "Well, it was an auspicious affair and got off with a big bang. Alan's father picked me up in his car with his two enormous Saint Bernards who liked to sit in your lap. When we arrived at the Alda home, I was greeted with a big spotlight that Alan had placed at the entrance to the house—to impress me. I was very impressed. He certainly knew how to make a young girl feel important." It is a practice he has kept up. He never forgets to bring his wife, Arlene, flowers when he comes home from the studio after a long day's shooting.

It was a grand birthday party in the true Hollywood tradition. There were dozens of kids. Alan treated his guests as one would a prized collection of treasured heirlooms. Of course, Alan turned the affair into a teenaged production extravaganza, encouraging everyone to perform in some way or other. He seemed to totally appreciate the talents of others and encouraged the kids to perform. Toni remembered that one young man could play the piano and joke. "Alan always joked, so it was a natural for him to exchange one-liners with the other boy, and it was a successful part of the party."

During the party several couples were encouraged to go into the den and dance alone—part of the girls' attempts to create a romantic setting. Jane and Leila manipulated Alan and Toni into, what must have been for them, the epitome of torrid romance. The young couple danced to the recording of "The Girl That I Marry," from *Annie Get Your Gun*. At one point in the song, the lyrics say, "and I'll whisper sweet nothings in her ear." At that point, Alan whispered in Toni's ear, "Nothing, nothing, nothing."

Romantic, indeed. But young love is young love and it is accompanied by the encumbrances of youth. The dance ended in a kiss. Toni will never forget that moment: "Yes, he kissed me—braces and all. I'd been taught never to embarrass a boy. So when Alan's lips met mine in that special moment, because of his mouthful of silver, his saliva ran down my face. Braces are not conducive to neat smooching. In order not to embarrass or make him feel self-conscious, I would wait until he turned his head before wiping my mouth on my sleeve." All part of growing up.

Jane, Leila, and Toni slept over that night while the other children went home at a proper hour. Jane knew all sorts of theatrical routines, so part of the night was taken up by the four doing skits. They had one routine with a guy (Alan) reading a newspaper. As the girl sashays by, Alan pops his head through an unseen hole in the paper. Very slapstick. Still, very funny because Alan had a natural ability to make slapstick acceptable. The boyish expression that he still retains helped him bring off routines with warmth and believability.

Toni says, "We took forever to get to bed that night. Jane and Leila wanted to see some romance. Alan tried to be romantic toward me—it was all very funny and ineffective.

"I woke up the following morning to the aroma of Italian cooking. Bob was in the kitchen singing and cooking breakfast. Joan did not come down until about noon in a flowing gown." Joan Alda was placed on a pedestal by her husband, who always indulged her as if they were still on a honeymoon.

Although he never liked being away from Joan and Alan for long periods of time, there were times when work dictated that he must be. On one occasion, while Toni was visiting, everyone was helping Bob pack to go to Chicago for a couple of weeks and Jane bounced about the room saying, "Chicago, Chicago," in a singsong voice, which seemed to annoy Bob simply because he didn't want to think about going without Joan and Alan.

When Bob was offered the role of Sky Masterson in the Broadway show *Guys and Dolls*, there was no such hesitancy because he would be taking Alan and Joan back to the East Coast with him. It was to be a permanent move and the end of Toni and Alan's puppy-love affair. Toni helped Alan pack for his migration to New York. It was not a tearful good-bye; Alan joked and Toni laughed at his humor. They swore true faith and promised to write regularly to each other. And they did—for quite a while. Also they spoke on the phone from time to time and Toni would call him from the airport in New York between planes as she traveled on to Italy on the numerous trips she made with her parents to Europe.

Then one day she got a "Dear Toni" letter from Alan. He was now attending a new high school where he had met and "fallen in love" with a girl named Jackie, who was in a play he had written for the school called *Love Is the Ticket*—his first effort at playwriting. He had given his new girl friend a ring because it was "the kosher thing to do." Toni stopped telling everyone she had a boyfriend and concentrated more on her schoolwork. It would be many years before she and Alan Alda would meet again, and under totally different circumstances they would reminisce about their childhood fun together.

It was inevitable that the Aldas would leave Hollywood. It was more a matter of when, rather than "if." For two years—even before the film was released—Warner Brothers had produced so much ballyhoo in the press and fan magazines about his performance as Gershwin that the fact that it did not live up to prerelease publicity did not enhance Bob Alda's stature in Hollywood. Jack Warner was never a man to voluntarily take blame for any failures at Warner Brothers Studios. He had underlings to take the blame for his miscues. Consequently, if *Rhapsody in Blue* was not a blockbuster at the box-office, then, in his place of power, he saw it as a failure on the part of his actor to properly captivate the movie-going public.

Alda was relegated to "just another contract player" at Warner Brothers. He could have stayed on in less-than-"A" starring roles, perhaps for the rest of his life, but it is unlikely that the studio would have spent more money to build him up as a major competitor against established romantic leads in the film industry.

Bob Alda never took kindly to being second anything and he was frustrated with the stance his studio had taken in regard to his future as an actor. Of the numerous films he made during his half dozen or so years in Hollywood, not one is remembered by even the most avid film fan except for *Rhapsody in Blue* and, for the monster cultists, *The Beast with Five Fingers*. Small wonder that he was so willing to make the move to Broadway when the opportunity presented itself. "I always considered myself more actor than movie star," he explained to one writer over lunch at Sardi's (after his phenomenal assault on Broadway in *Guys and Dolls*).

It was 1950 and the entertainment industry was undergoing a metamorphosis. Old acts were dying. Big bands were disbanding and those that remained were struggling to make ends meet financially. It was no longer economical to take big buses out on the road, and travel by train or plane was even more expensive. The same was true of legitimate theater tours. A show had to be solid gold on Broadway in order to feasibly play "the provinces." And the Great White Way was glittering with box-office gold as well as a number of dramatic flops. Names that meant something on the marquee were more important than great plays.

If war in Korea was psychologically a downer, it was exactly the opposite in terms of the entertainment world. At times of crisis the public has always turned to its show business stars for diversion. Katharine Hepburn, Jean Arthur, Helen Hayes, Ethel Waters, Julie Harris—all names known to carry a show—were emblazoned across the fronts of New York's legitimate theaters. Shirley Booth was wowing audiences with her performance in *Come Back Little Sheba* and would win not only dramatic accolades in New York, but also the coveted Oscar as best actress of the year in the screen version of the play. Ethel Merman played to standing room only in the fabulous musical *Call Me Madam*. The time was right for musicals. So it was a unique opportunity for Alda to be chosen to play Sky Masterson in Abe Burroughs and Frank Loesser's production of the Damon Runyon classic, *Guys and Dolls*. New York, like Hollywood, loves rumors and it was rumored that Alda was the producers' last choice to play the Masterson role. It was just that—rumor. Frank Sinatra was supposedly considered for the role (he did play another role in the film version), but that appears to be nothing more than conjecture. Sinatra, from about 1949 until 1953—when he appeared in *From Here to Eternity*—was having some tremendous voice problems (another rumor had it that he would never sing again). Nonetheless, he was never considered to have had a stage voice in the first place, so it seems doubtful that he would have been a likely choice for the Masterson role. In April of that same year (when *Guys and Dolls* opened), Frank reportedly lost his voice. On Wednesday night, April 26, 1950, he was appearing at the Copacabana—or rather he was scheduled to appear at the Copacabana. He opened his mouth to sing and nothing came out. He was replaced by Billy Eckstine. Later in the year, Walter Winchell reported that Sinatra had attempted suicide, so it was highly unlikely that producers of a new Broadway musical would risk money on a singer who was questionable in terms of both voice and emotional stability.

The show opened and was received enthusiastically by both the public and critics, who seldom seem to agree on anything. After reading the reviews the following morning, the Aldas knew they would not be returning to Hollywood in the near future, if ever. Alda shook his head in wonderment at the favorable turn of events. "If I had not been free-lancing, I would not have been able to accept the role in this musical fable of Broadway. When you are under contract to a studio, it is not possible to take over a stage role when opportunity knocks." He went on to win both the Tony Award and Donaldson Award. The *New York World-Telegram and Sun* reported:

Robert Alda caps a picture career and long service in second stem clubs with a solid, winning appearance as the gambler whose religion has a pretty face. Sooner or later everybody is going to say Alda resembles Cary Grant, so we might as well too. Is that bad? He knows how to belt a ballad and sings like Vaughn Monroe might on a clear day. I hope the theater hangs on to him.

With the renewal of his "celebrity status," he could now afford to live wherever he pleased. But it was because of fan adulation (which he was never crazy about) that he decided it would be easier for him to commute than for his family to be subjected to the daily rigors of Manhattan and fame. He and Joan found a house in Elmsford in Westchester County and a good Catholic school for Alan. Bishop Stepinac High School in White Plains was not coed, so Alan was back in the structured parochial atmosphere that he had so intensely disliked in the San Fernando Valley. He complained very little about his school to his parents, because he did not want to hurt his devout mother.

However, at school, Alan's tendency to speak his mind kept him in hot water with school authorities. Some have said he was quite witty and unappreciated by the hierarchy of the institution. Others saw him as a smart mouthed brat.

It was during his last year in high school that Alan's dramatic writing ability came into the forefront. An English teacher suggested he harness his talent and practically ordered him to write a play for the senior class. Interestingly enough, Alan accepted the challenge as if it were just another class assignment. His glibness and cockiness seemed to get him through any kind of confrontation or challenge. He has readily admitted that he was a "spoiled brat," which he hopes nobody will ever confuse with "Hollywood spoiled brat" because he detests the child-star syndrome. "There should be a law against child acting," he says. "It's a horrible condition for children. Stage mothers, for the better part, are absolute monsters who spend their time shoving and pushing their offspring toward bigger and better roles. It is sad to listen to youngsters sitting around discussing their parts, their makeup and hairdressers, and wondering if they look too old for the part. That can destroy a young person. I'm glad I never had the opportunity to become a child star of any variety."

Alda's resentment toward stage mothers comes from his experiences backstage while his father was onstage performing for servicemen and Alan stood nervously waiting to come out and do the Abbott and Costello routine with him. It was only a brush with acting at the tender age of nine and he was frightened at the thought of doing that in a competitive market on a daily basis.

As a student in New York, Alan was hardly one who made the dean's list with regularity, if at all. He attended a rather conservative institution, which, by that very fact, was also a very humorous environment in which to be educated. His forced entree into playwriting obviously hit the right nerve in his creative psyche, because during the hiatus between spring and the fall semester of his senior year he collaborated with a fellow student. The result of that effort was an original musical production called *Love Is the Ticket*, which must have endeared him to his English teacher and the school staff, since his first theatrical effort brought several hundred dollars into the school coffers. He had already acted in school plays, but this was a step in another direction of theater.

By this time, Bob Alda must have known that his young heir would try to emulate him, although it doesn't appear that he ever dreamed anyone would one day come up to him and say, "Aren't you Alan Alda's father?" After all, Bob was the star, not Alan.

Alan was never athletic or interested in competing in sports as other young men his age were. He felt more comfortable working on the school newspaper and soaking up all the information he could as a member of the drama club, and once he showed his bent toward the theater, his father was most generous with his counsel and advice.

At Bishop Stepinac, Alan seems to have had at least one close friend, Joe Colangelo, with whom he co-wrote *Love Is the Ticket* and other school productions. They also worked together in various capacities on the school paper, *The Shepherd*. There is an old adage in Hollywood that says, "Everybody loves a star," and Alan's senior year at Bishop Stepinac placed him in that category. His success as a budding playwright and literary genius propelled him into the magic circle of campus celebrity among both staff and students.

It is important to understand the setting in which Alan Alda emerged into his maturity. Chuck Berry was beginning to be noticed by white youngsters as the messenger of music yet to come (which must have been quite a shock to many of their parents, since black music was rarely if ever heard on "white" radio stations). Big bands were being replaced by personality singers and college prep types of groups such as The Four Lads. Frankie Laine sang of sentimentality and mule trains. For all practical purposes, it was the advent of a decade of peace and tranquility—a good atmosphere for a young actor-writer with the pacifist nature of Alan Alda.

If he was stretching his show business legs, they weren't allowed to do much traveling except to school and occasionally into New York with his father. Joan, who probably inherited her mother's strong sense of keeping family together, kept close tabs on Alan's whereabouts at all times. Much of her concern could have been motivated by his long siege with polio, but more than likely it was instigated by a gnawing loneliness that pervaded her existence at the time. The only time she spent with her husband and son together was when the theater was dark in New York, and even then Bob would often be caught up in interviews and other personal-appearance commitments. Alan, of course, was at school during the day, but he usually spent the better part of his weekends with Joan. He was concerned with her happiness, so consequently her apparent withdrawal into herself must have been cause for worry. No matter what his outside activities, which were almost totally connected with school, he devoted himself to his mother's well-being, both emotionally and physically.

If Alan was concerned with his mother's condition, she was almost paranoid about his. Skeptical of local physicians and dentists, she preferred the medical people in Los Angeles who had reassured her over and over during his long recovery from polio. Bob, who never seemed to think Alan was as ill as his wife did, may or may not have complained about the added expense of any return trips to California for medical attention, but he apparently complained from time to time that Joan wasn't permitting their son to be "one of the boys." Whatever misgivings he may have had fell on deaf ears as she mothered and protected Alan as much for her own security as for his. He may well have had his mother's "smother love" in mind when he told Susan Edmiston during an interview for *Vogue* magazine in 1976, "I wouldn't want to talk a lot about my feelings as a child; there still are people who could be affected by what I'd say. While there were plenty of positive things that I got from my mother and father, there were some things that had to be worked out, some unresolved feelings I had—that most people have toward their parents—that we transfer to other people. I think in a way it's everybody's lifework to understand the relationship they had with their parents when they were very young, before they could even verbalize their feelings."

The move to New York also apparently created a strain in the relationship between Bob and his adored Joan, which in turn filtered down to the very sheltered young Alan who, throughout his life, had always been protected by the security of a solid family situation. One might wonder if at that age and time in his life he was able to cope with the disintegration that was gradually taking place in his life. Although his parents, especially Joan, avoided any hint of dissension within the family, it seems reasonably certain that a young man with Alan's inherent sensitivities would have been aware that all was not harmony. It must have been difficult for him, brought up in the Catholic faith that marriage lasts forever, to face the possibility that his parents could *ever* go separate ways. Surely, when the actual split came, Alan was the biggest loser in divorce court. His own marriage patterns seem to prove his intent not to repeat the mistakes of his mother and father—or maybe just his father.

CHAPTER 4

Although Alan did have a few friends in high school, few, if any of them, were comparable to his show business chums. The Aldas had always entertained Bob's friends at home, almost all of whom were big names in the entertainment world, and predominantly comics and comedians. It is little wonder that Alan was able to bring so much finesse and expertise into the drama club at Bishop Stepinac: His teachers were vaudeville and Broadway's elite. Consequently, he always felt more at ease with show people. All the years of being tutored and pampered alienated him from the mainstream of life. Even in high school, he was the object of a pecking order that implied "Let's beat up on Alan—he won't hit back!" Had it not been for his dramatic bent and his mother's insistence that he get an education, Alan might have been able to convince his father that regular school was not for him. Apparently his love of the stage (even a high school stage) more than compensated for the abuse he received from classmates who didn't understand him. They had to respect his abilities, however, and this was truly a saving grace for the shy boy who seemed always to be "on" in a world that was understood by no one except himself— and, of course, his theater friends.

Alan still had female companionship in the form of his first leading lady who costarred with him in *Love Is the Ticket*. Like Toni, she was Italian. He was not one to play around. If he found a girl he liked, it was important to him and he did not see other girls. Outside Toni and the mysterious Jackie, there seems to have been only one other lady in his life prior to his marriage to Arlene Weiss. She was a girl from South Africa to whom he was engaged for a short time. He seems to have decided quite early in life that first things come first: Settle the matter of the girl friend and then go on to the mundane and/or exciting events of everyday living. Those early decisions are reflected by the manner in which he now conducts his life, both private and professional.

Sid Caesar, a very popular television comedian during the fifties, was Alan's absolute hero. He mimicked him, imitated him, and never missed an opportunity to watch him work, whether on the stage or in television. He once told *Los Angeles Times* movie columnist Joyce Haber: "In high school I wanted to be a comedian like Sid Caesar. But then I began to develop my taste for acting. Jokes are an avoidance of life. My father was very ambivalent about my ambitions. He taught me how to tell jokes but kept asking me not to be an actor."

Like any red-blooded American teenager, Alan ignored his father's advice and did as he pleased. His mother was spending more and more time alone. Alan would often perform with his father at various functions and was learning the fundamentals of being a comedian as well as a serious actor. Today, even his serious efforts at dramatics have comic overtones. Although she was a very private person, Joan could never stand being alone and often manufactured excuses to have local tradesmen from nearby Elmsford stop by the isolated Alda home just so she wouldn't be totally alone. At times she was near panic. She was respected and well-liked in spite of what some of the locals considered her "strange ways."

Bob and Joan's life had always been one of close harmony and in line with Italian family traditions. He held her in special esteem and she was expected to perform like an Italian's lady. For many years she had done just that—stayed in the background and permitted him the full stage. Always a gracious hostess, she had few friends of her own other than members of her own family, and some of them were continuously around. The people she entertained were her husband's associates and, later, Alan's school friends.

It seemed inevitable that unless she wished to become an absolute recluse, they would have to move back to the city. It is unclear, however, just whose idea it was that they give up the house in Elmsford and move back into Manhattan, but it is reasonable to assume that the trek was one last effort on both sides to try and salvage their tottering marriage—and perhaps to ease young Alan's mind as to the terminal nature of his home life.

The relocation in New York brought Joan back into the mainstream of life, but Bob Alda's course had been already decided. There would be no going back. First came the separation and friends choosing up sides. Bob's friends were as discreet as possible and Joan essentially had only her own family to turn to, having cut herself off from most outsiders. Her sister Jane became her most intimate confidante, as she had been for many years before the transition to New York from Hollywood. Bob was the man-about-town—seen at Sardi's and all the other stage-door delis and late-night spots. Although Alan was living with his mother, he spent most of his free time with Bob, and his loyalties were pressed. Always considered to be a mama's boy, he idolized his father. He tried not to take sides in their domestic squabbling.

Although Alan would just as soon have gone directly from Bishop Stepinac to acting, he was convinced by his parents to try college. It has been reported in print that his father talked him into college, but bearing in mind the past influence of his mother, it would be fair to assume that she had at least an equal voice in the decision. Alan was only sixteen when he applied for entrance to and was accepted at Fordham University. During the same year, he also ventured into summer stock with his father in Barnesville, Pennsylvania. If there had ever been any doubt where his future lay, it was resolved with that first real experience in theater. Most accounts say that Alan's first experience on the stage was with his father in a production of *Three Men on a Horse*, which may have been his Barnesville outing.

Much has been made about Alan being sixteen when he applied for entrance into and was accepted at Fordham University. Actually he was closer to seventeen, but still quite young. At the university, he had the opportunity to disassociate himself from family problems to some degree. He plunged into any and every kind of theatrical production available. His major was English literature—he was always thinking ahead. Acting was great fun, but his insatiable desire to express his own opinions lay lurking like an ingénue in the wings waiting for the star to collapse. One day he would be as well versed, or perhaps even more so, in writing as in acting. It is not unusual for him to wear several hats in a production today: producer, director, writer, and actor.

One of the most difficult situations a youngster finds himself faced with during a divorce is when one or both parents decide to tell the child how lousy the other parent is. It is one of the most common events in divorce and according to experts, the most devastating and traumatic to an impressionable and sensitive child. The turmoil with which Alan Alda was confronted when his parents separated and divorced could reasonably account for his almost-compulsive drive for privacy in his personal life and that of his family. One need not go behind the closed doors of Joan or Bob Alda's apartments in New York to know what they said about each other to Alan. Indeed not. It was emblazoned across the front pages of the New York dailies. And the battle was bitter. Alan and his mother apparently bounced from one abode to another, with Joan publicly berating her estranged spouse for nonsupport of herself and their son, now a college student. Still, Alan made every possible effort to maintain a balanced relationship between himself and his parents. From the very beginning, when Alan was only a baby, they had indulged him with love and a feeling of family security. He was made to feel that he would never have to suffer the hurt and pain that so many of his Hollywood contemporaries did. There were no boarding schools or stepparents. He did not have to read about marital battles between his parents in American newspapers arriving weeks later at some European prestige school for the

American wealthy. Nonetheless, though in his late teens, he was no better prepared for the onslaught between the two people he loved more than anybody else in the world.

If Joan made waves, Bob kept a low profile. Of course, the proverbial "other woman" later played an important part in Joan's accusations. She was a beautiful Italian actress who, not so coincidentally, eventually became the second Mrs. Robert Alda.

Much of this to-do went on while Alan struggled to involve himself in getting a college education. During his third year at Fordham, he attended the Sorbonne in Paris, escaping the marital confrontations between his parents for a brief respite. Bob, too, found an avenue of escape from Joan's accusations by scooting off to Italy, where he worked in television and films. It was shortly after his break with Joan that Bob, unemployed at the time (*Guys and Dolls* had moved away from Broadway), decided to accept an offer in Rome to star in a television series called "Secret File" (the working title had been "The Major Morgan Stories"). That was followed by a film that also went through a title change. Originally called *The Most Beautiful Woman in the World* (his costar was the Italian bombshell, Gina Lollobrigida), the title was watered down to *Beautiful but Dangerous*. It should have been called *Comedy of Misfits*. The actors all spoke their lines in whatever language they knew or suited their fancy, since the whole thing would later be dubbed to suit distribution of the picture worldwide. Vittorio Gassman said his lines in Italian *usually* (sometimes he lapsed into broken English); Gina, playing an Italian diva, kept to Italian; Alda delivered his speeches in English; and Anne Vernon, a well-known French film star, babbled in French, while playing an Italian character. Elke Sommer's husband, Joe Hyams—then an American journalist abroad—brought back stories to Hollywood about the sound stages that put the Tower of Babel to shame. While the thespians performed, the crew and workers cursed one another out in their various tongues in idioms that often only faintly resembled the native language.

It was during the filming of *Beautiful but Dangerous*, amid all the daily confusion on the set, that Alda's life became entangled once again, not in the divorce proceedings back in New York, but romantically with a young Italian actress. Recovering from an illness, she had checked in at the Tea Hotel where Bob Alda was taking rooms just to rest up from a whirlwind schedule of television and films. Ironically, the first meeting of these two soon-to-be lovers was as much a coincidence as that between Bob and Joan. It was the day before Christmas and as Flora, now feeling much better and recovering from her illness, hailed a taxi on the Via Veneto, the man of her dreams stepped out of another cab. Although it sounds quite corny, they both declare that their eyes met, locked, and it was an instant love to last forever. They did not, however, fall into each other's arms and profess undying love and devotion. Actually, she knew the face but couldn't place it, and he continued on into the hotel. A week or so later he let it be known that it had not been a slight on his part. He really liked this lady and went out of his way to make a striking impression on her. He asked one of the hotel officials to arrange an introduction. He did and Bob acted very casual about the whole thing. Flora did likewise. They were riot unlike two birds courting each other with nesting in mind. Not too close—and not too far. They often found themselves in the company of mutual friends and drifted slowly into long conversations that led to a more intimate relationship. There is little doubt that they both knew to what end their courses would take them. Flora did not, however, know all the entanglements Bob had left in New York with the unsettled business of his estranged wife.

The always flashy Bob Alda suddenly was playing the part of a shy swain. The gorgeous Italian signorina ate it up like candy. When Flora came down with a cold, Bob took on the self-appointed task of protector and daily visitor. From that point on, they were inseparable. Meanwhile Alan, quietly studying in Paris, came to Rome to meet his father's new girl friend. Bob assured Flora that she and Alan would get along famously. Flora was not so sure. She knew from conversations with his father that Alan was absolutely devoted to his mother, and she feared that he would consider her an intruder into the Aldas' family life. Truthfully, they were no longer a complete family and they all knew it—however reluctantly Joan accepted that fact. From all indications, she always hoped that Bob would come back to her.

In late 1955, Bob, Flora, and Alan returned to New York—Bob to work and Alan to continue his studies and later pick up a degree from Fordham University. He avoided discussing his father's new ladylove with his mother because he did not want to see her hurt further. Joan certainly must have asked questions of her son because she had not allowed "her desertion" by Bob to go unnoticed. For several years, her interviews with the media provided plenty of juicy gossip about the dissolution of her relationship and her poverty because of it.

Around Thanksgiving of that same year, the New York *Daily News* chronicled another episode in the "Saga of Joan" with the high-point headline: guys and dolls guy's doll is being evicted. According to Joan, she was being thrown out of her East Side hotel, bag and baggage and nineteen-year-old son Alan. Joan claimed Bob made big bucks; he denied it. Whether he did or didn't, he was seen in the expensive Broadway hangouts and was always known as a big spender. Additionally, he was footing the bill for Alan's expensive education.

Joan swore that he threatened to become permanently unemployed if she pressed for more money, which, incidentally, was a ploy the late Dick Haymes used on several of his wives in similar court actions seeking back alimony and child support. Whether Bob Alda made such threats or not is unclear, but he did continue to work.

During the mid-fifties it was considered a dastardly act to desert a wife and child, even if the child was a grown man. It was the peaceful doldrums of the Eisenhower administration—America's one last stab at recapturing the morality of the mid-Victorian era. A deserted wife's assault on a big star could cause him to crumble into the dust of the commonality. Whether or not Joan desired to destroy him because of hurt feelings or out of some imagined or real vindictiveness will never be known, but he was certainly put into an embarrassing position around the main stem of the Great White Way. Show people whispered behind menus and into napkins about the latest printed missives from Joan, and Bob had to know what they were thinking and saying. After all, he'd been in the business for a good many years and knew that entertainment folk spend a good deal of their leisure time gossiping and listening to gossip. During the run of *Guys and Dolls*, he made Sardi's, always one of the busiest gossip mills in the Big Apple, a home away from home. So Joan's efforts must have made some dent in her husband's social armor.

Often public sympathy is garnered by the tactics used by Joan, and for a while she accomplished just that—lots of sympathy. But she overdid it. Perhaps Bob was all the things she claimed—and more—but she beat him to death in the media and eventually people stopped taking her seriously. It was still a man's world, after all, and in many quarters Joan was pictured as a whining, nagging woman who had been overthrown for someone younger.

Early in 1957, Joan took Bob back into court and won nine hundred dollar-a-month payments for her support and care. Meanwhile, anxious to finish his marriage with Joan, Bob had, without her knowledge (even the press missed it) filed for divorce in Las Vegas, where he was appearing in *Guys and Dolls* at one of the Strip showrooms. When Joan finally found out about his action, she hit the roof and once again stood before the bench of a New York judge denouncing her husband and "the woman he plans to marry," whose expensive tastes would keep him broke and leave nothing for her support payments. By now Bob was appearing in a play in the East with Dorothy Lamour.

Joan's hysterics, dramatics, or whatever notwithstanding, the judge in Nevada was sympathetic to Bob's plight and granted him a divorce in November 1957. He had charged mental cruelty, and there are those who say it was more than just a catchall expression in this instance. Joan's last hurrah was just that—one last venomous toot that died on a weak note. From that point on, she faded into oblivion and has rarely been heard from since. She now lives alone quietly in a small cottage on a nondescript street in Burbank, California. Occasionally she speaks to a neighbor and is known from time to time to become melancholy and talk about the old days. It is rumored that her son paid for the house she lives in and supports her.

He and his wife, Arlene, have been seen stopping by for a visit, as one neighbor put it, "maybe a couple of times in the last year." When I was researching this book, I received a letter from someone who has known Joan throughout her years of self-imposed exile. It read in part:

I am appealing to you to treat her fairly in your book. ... In all the hoopla and gargantuan hype over Alan (and his father), Joan is very rarely mentioned, and usually in a throwaway manner.

She has been completely alone. More and more, age and emptiness and despair cloud and fog and befuddle. But sometimes I see flashes of clarity, and the person that appears deserves attention, however brief, and fair treatment.

It is to the credit of Alan and his father—and Flora Alda as well, for she certainly had good reason to dislike Joan—that they have not maligned or made any derogatory statements about Joan. For Bob, their twenty-five years of marriage must certainly have had great moments. He idolized this lady who loved to sleep until noon and then appear for breakfast looking like a beautiful vision in the eyes of her husband, who already had the table set and the orange juice poured.

However painful the memories of a split in the family are for Alan, he has kept the family skeletons in the closet and only on rare occasions has he let slip a word or line that would give an inkling to the pain he has kept locked away for so many years. No easy feat in a world filled with instant communications and electronic snoops that pry into the most secretive corners of our lives.

All of Alan's time was not spent trying to deal with the spaghetti tangle of his parents' problems. His final years in college were the breakaway he needed, and he thoroughly enjoyed himself in Europe. Returning from Paris by ship, he struck up an acquaintance with a fellow traveler who was the conductor of a symphony orchestra. Alan, always interested in anything classical, whether it be music, art, or literature, was quite impressed with the fellow, and when he invited him to come to his home in New York where he conducted chamber music concerts, Alan readily accepted. It was to be an evening of relaxation for Alda, who was coming home to attack his senior year at Fordham and also to make whatever contacts he could along Broadway. Theater was what he wanted, and so most of his spare time was spent auditioning and hanging around the legitimate houses, which was the same route his father had taken.

For the first time in his life he was "hanging loose," and that was not a situation familiar to him. It was soon to be reversed. At the concert he was to meet a young lady who would change the course of his future. Arlene Weiss was a no-nonsense girl whose dreams were of a career in classical music. Just as his father had cautiously wooed and won Flora, Alan pursued Arlene with a shy persistency. After their initial meeting, which was certainly paced conservatively, it was several weeks before he summoned the courage to invite her out for a night at the opera.

Even so, he was a bit more outgoing than he had been in the past, because during his stay in Paris he also journeyed to Rome, where he appeared on the stage with his father as well as on television with Bob in Amsterdam. It was during this period of time that he got to know and love Flora, recognizing that she was indeed the right person for his father.

If he was not as yet the total sophisticate, he was nevertheless a rather well-traveled young man with many theatrical credits due to the numerous theater and television appearances with his father. Evidence is ample that he acquired sophisticated tastes from his exposure to talents in many fields with whom he and his father came into contact after the family moved from Hollywood to New York.

Arlene Weiss, three years Alan's senior, was not only firm in her convictions and beliefs, but well-primed for life, with a solid academic and cultural background. When they met, she had just returned from a Fulbright year at Cologne Conservatory of Music in West Germany. A graduate of exclusive Hunter College, she was bright, witty, and ambitious. Her practicality and intellect attracted Alan probably as much or more than the usual charm and beauty. Arlene had a tendency to be in command of her own life, and after growing up under the strong maternal hand of Joan, Alan may have sensed a second mother figure in Arlene. She did, after all, come from a strong Jewish background just as family-oriented as his own had been. It would be difficult to ascertain if that was an attraction, but the attraction was magnetically strong from the beginning.

There were commitments they were both obligated to fulfill before venturing into any definite relationship. Arlene was a student performer at the National Orchestral Association in New York, while Alan, an R.O.T.C. member, was committed to a six-month hitch in the military following his graduation from Fordham. So romance was forced into a hiatus.

At Fort Benning, Georgia, Alan went into training as a gunnery officer. He was without a doubt one of the most misplaced trainees in military history. He hated being trained to kill. The rabbit incident kept popping up in his mind every time he took to the gunnery range, which was almost all day every day. The one bright ray in his daily life was Arlene. They wrote to each other daily, sometimes two and three times a day.

Work took Arlene south, too, but several hundred miles to the east of Fort Benning. She moved to Houston to play clarinet with the Houston Symphony Orchestra, then being conducted by the lion-maned, irascible Leopold Stokowski. Although separated, they knew that they would marry eventually.

Alan, a devout Catholic, never thought of leaving his faith to marry. It would have been an unconscionable act at that time and the final slap in the face to his mother, who was always important to him even though he spent more and more time with his father and Flora. He did everything he could to make his mother feel loved and needed. It was a difficult tightrope for him to walk.

Arlene understood the importance of a church wedding to Alan and did not haggle. She took instructions in the Catholic faith to accommodate him and to get their impending marriage off on the right foot. In those salad days, Alan was a devout churchgoer, embracing all the canons and sacraments of the Church.

When Alan's Italian traditions came into play, nowhere could he have found a more complementary partner than Arlene Weiss. By custom, Old World mores prevailed in the beginning of their union. Alan considered himself the breadwinner both in fact and artistically. Arlene would simply have to forget symphony orchestras and learn to play household music. Arlene, following the centuries of Jewish role-models before her, acquiesced to her husband's desires and to all practical career purposes, she put away her clarinet. In its place she took up cookery and housekeeping. All the dedication and devotion she had shown toward music now went into making this traditional marriage a happy one. Theirs might as well have been a marriage arranged in the old country.

Alan's dedication to faith has changed definition over the years. At the time of his marriage to Arlene Weiss, he based his religious commitment on faith. Not so very long ago, with hindsight vision, he said, "I've made so many moral commitments, I believe, because I was a guilty Catholic."

Following their marriage in Houston, the newlyweds deserted the South, both Georgia and Texas, and moved on to the bright lights of Broadway and Manhattan. They hoped the City would offer more security than the grassy knolls and picket fences of southern comforts.

During the early months of their marriage, Alan and Arlene lived in a midtown Manhattan apartment—one unlike that of his parents in the sense that there was not a constant stream of relatives parading through on a day- by-day basis. Even now, as Alan expresses regret over Arlene's subjugation to his career during those early days, she has never publicly voiced any misgivings about her choice. Alan says they have talked about it quite a bit, but she has been somewhat the Sphinx in her opinions on the subject.

New York did not immediately offer success. It was not long until Arlene was pregnant with their first child and Alan was struggling with part-time jobs to support himself, his wife, and a forthcoming child. He also had to provide bus fare and lunch money as he traversed the theatrical district during his "free" time looking for anything offered in the world of entertainment.

Arlene was and is a practical and frugal woman. She knows how to save a penny and a dollar. In those days there were more pennies than dollars, so, with all her practicality, she took on some music students. It gave her a chance to be involved with her music, and still have time to be a homemaker and wife. While Alan was working or looking for work, she taught youngsters the beauty of lilting notes.

Alan, of course, was no stranger to Broadway. Since high school, he had been a familiar figure by his father's side in thespian haunts. Also, with little fanfare, he understudied Don Murray in Thornton Wilder's *The Skin of Our Teeth* while still in college. It was a short-lived backup however. The play, unlike the original in 1942 starring Tallulah Bankhead and Fredric March—and newcomer Montgomery Clift—which won for Mr. Wilder the Pulitzer Prize, ran only a few weeks and then abandoned New York (or was abandoned by New Yorkers) for a tour in the hinterlands.

It must have been difficult for Arlene to accept such a dramatic change in life-style. Both her parents had worked and worked hard. Her father was a lithographer and her mother had always spent long hours as a seamstress. Although they were not wealthy, they were able to send their daughter to Germany to study classical clarinet. Once they were in New York, however, a continuous string of part-time, sometimes jobs occupied Alan Alda's working hours. He simply would not allow any employment to interfere with his acting ambitions. He budgeted his time in order to pound the sidewalks of New York, besieging agents and casting directors for any crumb of a part that might further his career. He would scrounge the fast-food stands looking for the cheapest sandwiches for his lunch. An inexpensive meal was his idea of wealth, he revealed during an interview in 1980.

His employment for wages during those lean and hungry times were varied and somewhat menial, and mostly transient situations: cabdriver, doorman, clown at small business openings. He may have picked up some sound advice from the late film actress Jayne Mansfield, who once said, "I cut ribbons at openings because it is a chance to be seen." Theoretically, one never knows when an agent may wander by and find you the perfect type for an upcoming part. A face in the crowd means nothing. Once at a supermarket opening where he was working as a clown and had several dozen balloons on strings, a small coterie of hoodlums attacked him. He released the gas-inflated objects and ran for his life. A lousy salesman by his own admission, he made an attempt at selling baby pictures and often did not make enough money for his lunch. That never mattered because he would chuck selling for the day and make the rounds.

Although Alda gives the impression of being a very laid-back man, he has never practiced that image. He has always been a go-getter. A man who loves attention, being right, and being in control. Even with a very famous father, it was no easy task for Alan to crash Broadway. Being the child of a celebrity can be, and often is, as much a handicap as being unknown.

He ran into two main confrontations when trying out for a play. Initially, of course, there was the curiosity; even producers are curious about the offspring of celebrity. Curiosity, then, will get you in the door for a look-see, but it is talent or the lack of it that will rule the day. Still, it boils down to a pair of negatives. If you are the son or daughter of a famous star it is generally figured that, one, you are pulling rank simply because of your famous parent or, two, you are taking work away from someone who really needs it. The incorrect assumption is that you are a spoiled brat with nothing to do and auditioning out of boredom rather than any sincere desire. Such jealousies abound in show business and the children of stars have time and again expressed their hurt and anger over such unfair treatment.

It was no different with Alan. He ran into the same stone wall other celebrity children have encountered. The difference between him and others of his breed was that he was determined to use his background in a positive way rather than to allow himself to be browbeaten by petty resentments. Having been rather spoiled as a child, it might figure that he would have thrown a few temper tantrums, but he did not. Perhaps always having been catered to and given so much he was ready to fight for what he wanted simply because he was used to having it.

Those first few years of marriage were transitory for the Aldas. While Arlene was carrying their first daughter, Eve, Alan managed to finagle a Ford Foundation grant to the Cleveland Playhouse. Since Alan's career came first, Arlene gave up her music teaching in New York, her obstetrician, and their apartment to make the trek west to Ohio along with their unborn child. With the move went the bulk of their income—Arlene's earnings from teaching. She had become the mainstay of their existence as Alan wore out shoes and patience searching for "career" work.

Alan was known as his father's son. His face was familiar off Broadway as well as at certain television studios. While in Cleveland, living quietly by Lake Erie and applying himself as a student of repertoire company productions with the Cleveland Playhouse, Alan and Arlene had long hours in which to reflect on their past and think about the future. It was a time of evaluation and change. A new morality entered Alan's life. He has expressed himself as being apprehensive with his decision to return to New York after fulfilling his military obligations rather than making an effort with the Abbey Theater in Houston, which was also a well-known repertoire company. It would have given Arlene the opportunity to continue with the Houston Symphony and to have perhaps established her professional reputation in music—as she has recently with photography. Although he has expressed sorrow at placing his desires ahead of his wife's, he now has the advantage of hindsight. He recently said, "Yes, I feel guilt, but you must understand that we were victims of sex stereotyping." Arlene came out on the short end of such social orientation, but was obviously so in love with her husband that she didn't notice.

It was during their years in Cleveland that Alan apparently abandoned the Catholicism he had so long embraced and from whose roots he had evolved. Whether Arlene's questioning her own Judaism influenced him away from the Church is difficult to determine, but something motivated his rejection. He has said, "After our first baby came, I abandoned the formalities of the Catholic church. Although I had practiced my religion meticulously as I had been taught from infancy to do, I found that I now had questions that couldn't be answered by the Church and could no longer accept concepts that I had always taken for granted simply because I was told to do so."

Perhaps, but although his daughters have since been brought up in a loosely associated "free thought" style of religion, the family nevertheless celebrates religious holidays—both Catholic and Jewish. In spite of Alda's unanswered theological questions, his children have had a religious upbringing that embodied both the Judeo and Christian ethics.

Alan's training at the Cleveland Playhouse was his first real excursion into theater without the nearness of his famous father and the comfort of his counsel and explanations of the pitfalls of acting. Not only was he faced with doing a solo, far from the comforts of the Hollywood Canteen where he and Robert Alda mimicked Abbott and Costello, but he had the added responsibility of marriage and children. Married in 1957, his three daughters arrived in typical Old World fashion: Eve—1958, Elizabeth—1960, and Beatrice—1961. It has been said of Alda that he dedicates himself totally to any project he is involved in. Family was something he took seriously, and with dead aim he attacked the matter with great dedication.

Very little is known about Alan's residency with the Cleveland Playhouse, primarily because he was still a novice in theater there.

Having a famous movie and stage star father did not endow him with talent. It was only background for an untried young man seeking a career in the theater.

With a growing family, Alan could not afford to remain a "promising student" indefinitely. After three years in Cleveland, he, with Arlene's concurrence, decided it was time to return to New York and make another run on the theater. By now Alan was also writing during his spare time and had amassed quite a portfolio of articles, skits, and plays. He seemed to feel that if he was not successful in one medium of theater, then perhaps his talent lay in another. As time would eventually reveal, he was equally adept in many facets of entertainment and the entertainment industry. There was always the possibility that by wearing so many hats he might burn out early. In some men's makeup such might have been the case, but not with Alda. He was a young man in hot pursuit—even if he didn't exactly know for sure where that chase might lead. He had energy to burn, which endowed him with the glow of optimism.

New York held his future, if he indeed had one, and he assaulted Manhattan with all the zeal and industriousness of the colonials attacking the New World.

CHAPTER 5

If Alan's emoting was not setting the theater world on fire, he was rooting himself deeply in family life. Home, wife, and children were his mainstays as a man and human being. His love for Arlene has always been unquestionably the number-one force in his emotional existence. She was always there and always accommodating. Yet, they did have the usual problems of newlyweds for several years after their marriage in Houston.

No matter how much in love young people may be, the coming of children and lack of steady income on the part of the husband will create chinks in even the strongest armor. The Aldas were no exception. Both Alan and Arlene have spoken openly about their early years, not only of the ambitions and hopes but also of the realities in bringing up a family with no certain economic future.

"Although we didn't discuss it at the time, we both just assumed that our relationship would be based on tradition as we knew it from our families." Both Jewish and Italian families were steeped in tradition, so the guidelines were there to help Alan and Arlene along the path toward marital stability. But tradition often proved to be a handicap. Arlene once said, "We knew more about our families and their traditions than we did about each other." It was assumed that she would play the role of nice Jewish mother and wife, filled with love for husband, children, and home, whereas Alan was expected to be the breadwinner who would staunchly march forward to protect the family hearth while providing adequate nourishment at the table and a roof over the family's abode. Arlene accepted her role of mother first and foremost, with any thought of career secondary, if at all.

Although she expresses little or no rancor over the role she played during those early days of their marriage, occasionally resentment creeps into any conversation she has about the beginnings of the Alda family life. "I wanted children. I think any woman does, but let me tell you," she points out, "kids are a difficult chore. Bringing them up properly is no part-time occupation. I wanted to do other things. I knew my potential, but felt I couldn't step out into the creative world or work force to do those things because I was a mother and wife with three daughters to raise. I had job offers to play with orchestras, but always I had to pause and ask the question, Can I leave the girls with someone else?" Inevitably she always reached the same conclusion: She could not. Rather than work only when Alan was available to be with their children, she chose to give up work altogether.

The price she paid for such a decision was to bury her frustration and anger under the facade of total motherhood, something she would have to deal with more directly in years to come.

Alan, in retrospect, appreciates now the fact that when something is for nothing or if you sacrifice (or think you do) something for someone else, the payment is often harsh and sooner or later must be made by the beneficiary of such concessions.

As she tackled what seemed to be endless stacks of diapers and baby clothes, her real base of support came from the knowledge that she, indeed, had opted for this condition, that no matter how much resentment she may have nourished, it was, after all, her choice. She related her feelings in interviews to numerous writers, long after the fact of course. She felt trapped, while Alan was a free spirit enjoying the outside world. In a marriage that both entered with the agreement that both partners had equal status in the pact, she saw Alan enjoying more and more of the benefits and herself often ensnared by mundane daily chores.

The Aldas were no sooner relocated in New York than Alan picked up the reins of Broadway and once again began his determined siege on agents and producers. With the years of training in Cleveland securely behind him, he had more foundation than ever to pursue his goal—stardom. He accepted any and all parts that were available.

The time was right for a young man with Alan's ambitions. He may have been the only person in the world who believed he was the "nice young man" that mothers would one day pray that their own sons would emulate. However, Broadway, not unlike Hollywood, was and is a dream factory. It is not the actors' dreams that come true; they merely carry out the fantasies of writers, producers, and moneymen (or "angels" as they are known along Broadway).

Alan's early adventures in television include supporting roles in the old "Sergeant Bilko" series, which starred comedian Phil Silvers; "The Nurses"; "Route 66," which brought television fame to Martin Milner; "The Trials of O'Brien"; and several others, which may have given him acting experience but were nothing of a nature that would have made him stand out. Even in one of the numerous Broadway and off-Broadway productions he had previously acted in, it was only in a scene where his clothes accidentally caught fire that he received personal notice.

It can honestly be said that Alan was paying his dues to his craft on a long-term installment plan.

During this period Alan appeared in *Compass*, a stock production in Hyannisport, Massachusetts, where the Kennedy clan ruled socially and sat in judgment on cultural affairs. If they did not praise Alan's efforts, they certainly did not pan him—a plus for any entertainer striving for recognition at the commencement of John F. Kennedy's "Camelot."

When he was a mere teenager and had first decided that acting was the career he wanted, he later recalled that he "would be in anything just to work or to be seen, although I can't bear the idea now of taking an audience's time for something that isn't worthwhile." He proffered that "a theatrical experience is something you can take home with you and savor for all your life." He related the feeling as being as beneficial as a shot of penicillin.

His work with *Second City* was extremely beneficial, since it gave him confidence in his own ability, although he looks back at old home movies and sometimes cringes at the gangly, awkward kid he sees himself as at that point in his career, marveling that anyone would have paid to see him perform—but they did. With *Second City* he learned to relate to other actors in a situation without worrying about relating what he was doing to anything in the past or some unknown role he might have in the future.

Although he appeared in numerous plays and productions, Alan made his official Broadway debut in *Only in America* in 1959. A *Pictorial History of the American Theater* (Crown, 1971) doesn't even mention the play. That oversight hasn't concerned Alan, since he, as do most actors, considered each and every experience a learning one rather than a failure or "flop." Actors need tough exteriors. Alda is no exception.

Of those early days he says, "The experience was invaluable, not only as a person but as an actor. I began to realize what the body can attain at the command of the imagination."

Only in America was an interracial off-Broadway effort that dealt with black/white social relations in a series of vignettes and was considered a major work by many critics, especially in terms of black theater. Alan's sense of social justice was being honed and refined. He had spent his military duty in Georgia, the heart of segregationist America, but if he had any compassion or deep feelings about injustice to southern blacks at the time, there is no recorded evidence of such feelings. Working with black actors gave him an opportunity to deal with a different race and culture.

Ossie Davis, a fine black actor, had written a play called *Purlie Victorious*, primarily as a star vehicle for his wife, Ruby Dee. Both Ossie and Ruby were familiar faces to the screen as well as the Broadway stage. They were proved box-office draws to both the white and black movie- and theatergoer. When the play arrived on Broadway on September 21, 1961, the cast, in addition to Ossie and Ruby, included other established black actors such as Godfrey Cambridge, Roscoe Brown, and Helen Martin (who went on to the musical version, *Purlie*). Alan Alda, as Charley Cotchipee, a well-meaning but not too bright young man of the South during the days of slavery, once again was placed in the position of playing with and off blacks in a play that spoofed slave owners and stereotyped overseers.

Alda was beginning to identify with minority rights and was finding there was a certain critical and emotional acclaim to be gained by supporting the underdog—a lesson that has served him well over the years and garnered untold reams of publicity in his favor. Critics rarely attack or find fault with anyone supportive of minorities. If Alda took this path out of compassion for the deprived in our society or for more selfish publicity reasons, he has both received that publicity *and* been a great help to minority causes.

Alan received good reviews for his role in *Purlie Victorious* and was well-liked by his fellow cast members. Helen Martin remembers Alan with warmth and fondness:

Alan hasn't changed as far as I'm concerned. Different people have different ideas, but I read everything about him and he is a beautiful person inside. Alan's dressing room was on the other side of mine and someone told me that his father was Robert Alda, the famous movie star. That just blew my mind because I had always been crazy about Robert Alda. I remembered him from "The George Gershwin Story" (*Rhapsody in Blue*) and thought he was the living end. I knew all the old movies because throughout my years on Broadway I spent all my afternoons after rehearsals or between shows in the Times Square theaters. Movies were my thing.

I found Alan to be a very nice man. He was friendly and warm and very cooperative. His warmth strikes you right away. He made you feel that you had known him all your life—like a member of your own family. His girls were very small. He had already settled his family into the small New Jersey town of Leonia and commuted into the city every day for the play. I knew his wife, Arlene, and she, too, was very folksy—just like Alan. I remember thinking what a lovely couple they made—so considerate and concerned for others.

Alan took direction well in those days. Howard Da Silva directed the play and was a stickler for players being on time, especially for rehearsals. Many times you don't have to be at the theater until your scene is being rehearsed. Alan was always there ahead of time, listening to the other actors, getting the right perspective of his own role, and was generally a delight to work with. Oh, occasionally he would forget a line or fluff something, but then all actors do that. It is part and parcel of live entertainment.

Nobody in the production made waves. We were all professionals who were there to put on a quality production, so there were no problems. Nothing that could be considered "the star attitude" that I found in the musical version of *Purlie.*

We did have one problem—or it was a problem for me, in a way—during the run of *Purlie Victorious.* Phil Rose, the show's producer, was also producing another show at the same time and putting money into that production, which meant we began to get cuts in salary. At one point, I was down to eighty dollars a week. Although Phil was more into the new show, we were continuing to carry the crowds that flocked to see our show. The audiences still got excited. It was a funny play. It was a comedy with a subtle underlying message. Very clever. Alan seemed to sense the meaning from the first. He understood the black mentality, both on the stage and off, which helped keep harmony with the cast. He didn't do that all by himself, of course, but he contributed in a large way. He was white and it would have been very easy for a white actor to permit his ego to get in the way of the purpose of the show. Alan never did that. He knew who the stars of the show were and he played his role.

I don't think Alan was into activism at that time. If he was I certainly didn't see it and he never made an issue of that. Alan played the son of a plantation owner with deep feelings about people. I think Alan just played himself, because he reflects that concern for others all of the time.

Helen Martin echoed the sentiments of others in the cast and production company, perpetuating the "good guy" image of Alda. She was somewhat incensed that Barbara Walters, interviewing Alan on a television program, tried to paint him as a sex symbol. "He's no sex symbol," Helen chirped. "He's a family man who goes home to his wife and family at night."

Purlie Victorious was a very successful play, which ran for 261 performances. Alan would go on to repeat his role in the film version, *Gone Are the Days*(1963). Although he is considered by many to be a serious dramatic actor, most of Alda's roles have had serious/comic underpinnings. Even at that point in his career, he was able to deliver devastating social statements in the guise of comic relief. He has proved himself a master of subtle innuendo.

Sometime during this period in his life Alan sought the help of a psychologist. It is the one subject about which he is more reluctant to speak than his private family life. He has denied ever seeking any psychological help, only to have his memory jogged by interviewers. In an interview with Carey Winfrey of *The New York Times Magazine*, which appeared on April 19, 1981, after a tiresome day's shooting on *The Four Seasons*, Winfrey asked Alda about his sessions in psychotherapy. Alan quickly denied he had ever been in therapy. "I never had any therapy," he said flatly. Winfrey reminded him that it had been written about previously. Alan responded, shortly, "I did have some therapy; that's right. Yeah. For a short time." The subject was immediately dropped by Alda. But Winfrey did not forget and a few days later when they were discussing his childhood illnesses, he got Alan to open up a bit more on the matter. Alan confessed that his chubbiness as a child, caused by a thyroid deficiency, and of course his bout with polio had created deep emotional problems. The parents of other children—ignorantly expecting him to contaminate their offspring—kept their children from playing with Alan. This rejection and isolation complicated his already difficult situation as the son of a celebrity. He was put in a spotlight, which was hard for someone so young, and it carried over into adult life. Still, he denied that was the cause of his seeking therapy. He contended that his therapist dealt only with the present and he couldn't remember what had brought him to therapy in the first place. He ended the conversation with a bit of the Alda wit: "I think that's between me and Sigmund Freud." It is a classic example of Alda wanting to be in total control at all times. He often cuts interviewers short when he feels they have invaded a domain that does not belong to the public.

In any event, Alan was now on the road to a successful career. *Purlie Victorious*, although not a star role, gave him the push he needed. It was not long until other offers were coming in, and remembering all the lean days and the uncertainties of the past, he had difficulty turning down any offer. By the end of the play in 1961 Alan was three times a father. By the time his youngest daughter, Beatrice, was born, Alan was finally in a position to make a living and support his family without having to worry about finances. He was not an overly indulgent person so far as material things were concerned, nor was Arlene. They found great comfort and enjoyment from just being a family, being together in their cottage, with its picket fence and flowers, in suburban New Jersey—away from Manhattan traffic and the race for survival and recognition. It was, indeed, the best of all worlds—a condition that Alan has endeavored to maintain over the years with a great deal of success.

Alan's work in *Compass* brought him recognition as a man who was as easily adept at political satire as he was with musicals or serious drama. He was astride a horse of confidence—a steed that gave him a mature (if not totally secure) attitude toward his craft. It is not outside the realm of possibility that he remembered the insecurities and disappointments endured by his father in the motion-picture jungle before he attained recognition and success as a serious actor on Broadway in *Guys and Dolls.*

Long before he became a celebrity, Alan and Arlene decided that theirs would be a normal family and that their daughters would be brought up the same as any other three children who have decent, loving homes. That was not a difficult task in those early days while he was busy establishing himself as an actor and Arlene was striving to maintain a sensible budget, living within the means afforded by Alan's paychecks. The girls were never overly indulged in a material sense. Alan has said, "I've always thought that large doses of love and attention and understanding have much more lasting value than new toys, which soon start collecting dust from lack of use." Both parents balanced their time so that the children were never neglected, even after Arlene became engrossed in activities outside the home. Their unpretentious cottage on a quiet little street in Leonia, New Jersey, was the perfect setting for a man who had such a compelling desire to be just "a plain Joe" when he came home from the bright lights of Broadway or the klieg-lit Hollywood movie sets. There is a quality to Alda's personality that causes him to ask the question, Why not have the cake and eat it, too? He loves the limelight. He loves attention and yet at the same time he seems to entertain the desire to say to the public, "Here I am—but don't touch."

Being recognized by his own peers and by the critics must have given him a great sense of satisfaction. Until *Purlie Victorious,* he had always been "Robert Alda's son." Now he was Alan Alda and people would often ask, "I wonder if he's related to that movie star—what's his name—you know—that Alda guy who played Gershwin back in the forties."

It is difficult to be the child of any highly successful person, but the most trying childhood of all is to be the offspring of a famous actor or actress. There is frequently a built-in love/hate relationship between the child of a celebrity and the world. The children of stars are expected to be without flaws, living up to the image projected by their famous parents. If they look for employment outside the entertainment industry, they often conceal their real identity. That is not simply because they do not want to be identified as the child of a star, but employers often feel they don't need the job and are depriving someone who really does need employment from finding it. On the other hand, if they desire to follow their parents into "the business," they are just as likely to be considered "freaks," little more than curiosities.

Because Alan traveled down that pathway himself, he tried every means possible to protect his children from being stigmatized by who he was. Because of that quirk, being a celebrity parent, it is possible that he overdid the "normal childhood" syndrome and created a vacuum wherein his children's lives were "too normal."

Nonetheless, when the girls were small, it didn't matter that much because they were not exposed to the outer world as the children of a star. Alan was climbing, but he wasn't there by any means. His name was not as yet a household word. He was a working actor, making progress, who had goals in mind that he not only hoped to attain. He had little serious doubt that he would do just that. (Recently it was estimated that Alda's annual income now is in excess of $2 million. In typical latter-day Alan Alda humor, his response to that was, "I'm worth every penny of it.")

It is quite possible that Alan had no serious psychological hangover from his childhood and was having greater early success at family than career, as he suggests. Perhaps he was doing nothing more than adjusting to maturity with a creak and a groan from time to time coming from his emotional timbers. That these adjustments came when they did was a good omen, because Alan's future was about to take one of its several giant leaps with a staccato pace over the next few years. His creative soul had reached the edge of the cliff. It was either leap to fame or fall.

CHAPTER 6

New York in the early sixties was alive with enthusiasm for British imports. This was never so true as it was in the make-believe world of show business. The Beatles were making their mark in music. Although they had not as yet made their first triumphant tour to the United States, where they would pack Shea Stadium with their concerts, their music filled the air on radio and jukebox. Kids were abandoning such rock stalwarts as Elvis Presley and Little Richard for The Beatles and other new groups with unlikely names such as The Rolling Stones, Herman's Hermits, and The Monkees, an American group patterned after the Beatles.

Still, the legitimate stage traditionally sought its own path of originality and "new statements." Movie stars were joining Broadway actors in the ever-growing transition to that dreaded medium, television, where one could receive instant recognition and become an overnight star. Television was employing more members of Actors Equity and The Screen Actors Guild than were the parent unions. It became increasingly popular to carry an AFTRA (American Federation of Television and Radio Artists) card. It was the new key to steady employment for hundreds, perhaps thousands, of actors and their support groups.

In 1963 Hollywood beckoned Alan to reprise his role of Charlie Cotchipee in the film version of *Purlie Victorious*, renamed *Gone Are the Days*. The new title, which was the name of an old Negro spiritual, spoofed the original Broadway production, making some light of the stereotype that blacks only know spiritual music. In the play it was really hammed up. Something got lost in the transition because the film barely rated a trickle in the mainstream of motion pictures.

Alda's acting has always *appeared* to be comedic, even when that was not his intent. He is a ham. Even when receiving a prestigious award, he cannot resist doing something ridiculous on the podium—standing on his hands, cracking vaudeville jokes. One feels that he has a sense of not deserving any accolades and does cartwheels across the stage more out of embarrassment than any effort to garner more attention. The other side of this assumption is the fact that he is an actor who, like most actors, is "on" around the clock—even when he is screaming for privacy and "no more pictures, please!"

Perhaps, because his father's early Hollywood career had been so disappointing, Alan saw the stage as his particular forte. After all, when Bob Alda came to Broadway, he was wined and dined and became the toast of the town. Following the debacle with Warner Brothers, Bob Alda's appearance and acclaim on the legitimate stage made him look like a brand-new discovery. Hollywood did not exactly roll out a red carpet for Alan when he came out to film *Gone Are the Days*. Rejection is always just around the next corner in the motion-picture industry, and Alan has, by his manner and actions, expressed a great fear of rejection or slight. Again, that attitude can probably be tracked back to his childhood days when he was stigmatized as the child of a celebrity and shunned when he was ill with polio.

In Hollywood, next to image, winning is everything. Alan did not project himself as a winner on the screen. Still, his trek into the land of celluloid magic was not without merit. Alan's ambition beyond acting was to write. Even in high school, writing school plays, he considered himself first and foremost a writer, not a clown. Generally, there is more status in writing—being the man behind the power that is projected on the screen or stage. Alan rubbed elbows with writers. It is possible, although not certain, that his next Broadway assignment was germinated in Hollywood.

Bill Manhoff, a pixieish, charming young man, was working in Hollywood. Although he maintained an apartment in New York, Bill's headquarters was essentially Hollywood. He wrote television situation comedies—"The Donna Reed Show,"

"The Real McCoys"—the light fare that has always been the mainstay of television, catering to what one television executive once explained as "the twelve-year-old American mind." Bill had anything but a twelve-year-old mentality. He was bright, articulate, and had a tremendous social consciousness. Retrospectively, it seems quite logical that he and Alan Alda would become involved in some manner.

Alan's ability to innovate a role was establishing his trademark. He could be psyched up to any character in a matter of minutes. Bill Manhoff, between episodes of the silly television fare that was paying his bills, sat down and furiously clicked out a play on the keys of his old manual typewriter. The result was a play entitled *The Owl and the Pussycat*, the improbable story of love between a hooker and a sophisticated, literate New Yorker.

The male lead was ideally Alan Alda material. It would later become a film starring George Segal—another actor with a clown inside—and the irrepressible Barbra Streisand. When Alan came to Broadway with the play, his costar was the beautiful black actress, Diana Sands. Not that black hookers were any more abundant than their white sisters, but the twist was the kind of innovation that Alan loved. His ability to work with black actors was well known.

Alan now threw himself into an incredible work schedule. He had something to prove to Hollywood. His confidence in himself was not shaken by the innocuous presentation and reception of *Gone Are the Days*. Alan's ability as a political satirist, once limited to the party circuit (and in those early days he and Arlene went to a good many cocktail parties because it was important to be seen) was put to a more practical use.

A brash, young, wry-witted talk-show host from England, David Frost, brought his own particular brand of satire to the United States. In January of 1964, "That Was the Week That Was," which became more familiarly known to television viewers as "TW3," premiered on NBC television. The Frost style of humor was biting and often downright insulting, with the current headline hunters becoming targets for his darts. He assembled a cast for the show that included Alan Alda, giving Alan his first sustaining television audience. The irreverence of the show's format and host made it an immediate hit. Still, it was a show before its time and the Nielsen boxes showed a decline in popularity after a while. It was, however, a forerunner of Rowan and Martin's extremely successful "Laugh-In," which, although it did not have the acrid venom of "TW3," did much more to tickle the television viewer's funny bone. For Alan, it was a bonanza. On Broadway he was also appearing in *Fair Game for Lovers*, a comedy which the critics found only mediocre. Alan, nonetheless, was singled out for particular acclaim. He was, according to several reviewers, managing to make something out of what often was weak material and showed a great deal of promise for the future.

The personal plaudits did not go unnoticed by Broadway producers. Alda was for the first time reaching audiences in more than one area of entertainment: movies, television, and stage. When Phil Rose, who had produced *Purlie Victorious*, began to cast *The Owl and the Pussycat*, he knew that Alan was right for the male lead, that of Felix Sherman, the intellectual whose experimentation with a nonintellectual black hooker leads to love. It was a script filled with improbables, the kind of role that was written with Alan's ability to play subtle comedy. He could certainly look back and thank his father for the opportunity to do Abbott and Costello routines as a youngster because even in subtle comedics, timing is the most important ingredient—next to talent, of course. There was no doubt in Phil Rose's mind that Alan was talented.

Diana had created the role of Beneatha in Lorraine Hansberry's prizewinning play about black struggles to integrate suburban housing patterns, *A Raisin in the Sun.* She went on to reprise that same role in the film version and was a marketable product in both black and white audiences. She had appeared in the off-Broadway productions of *Brecht on Brecht* and *The Living Premise.* She had won a Theater World Award for her 1962 emoting on Broadway in *Tiger, Tiger, Burning Bright.* Some critics thought her greatest performance had been given in James Baldwin's biting *Blues for Mr. Charlie.* Diana had appeared in several films as well, including *Raisin in the Sun* and *Ensign Pulver.* No assignment had pleased her more, however, than the female lead opposite Alan in *The Owl and the Pussycat.* She felt she had finally overcome the stigma of race, appearing as the female lead in a Broadway production opposite a white male. "This," she said, "is the first Broadway play in which I was cast as a person rather than a racial type. I love doing it. When it's over, the owl and the pussycat leave hand in hand to dance by the light of the moon."

The play tried out for three weeks at the Bergen Mall Playhouse in Paramus, New Jersey. Only *New York Times* critic Howard Taubman had less than praise for the production. He wrote that it was "dry, brittle comedy," comprised of essentially "slick comic writing." But Alan and Diana's performances won all the other major critics' approval and the rest became history.

For the first time in a career that had wavered back and forth in a lukewarm womblike atmosphere, Alan had broken the barriers. He was now legitimately, if not firmly, established as a star on Broadway, just as his father had been twelve or so years earlier in *Guys and Dolls.* It was extremely important for him to have roots firmly established in legitimate Broadway theater. He was now an accredited theatrical actor with all the prestige such a position implied. He was not something pieced together out of celluloid with perhaps the better elements left strewn on the cutting-room floor.

It did not upset Alan that while Diana Sands was nominated for a Tony Award (which went to someone else), he was ignored. His delight in having a Broadway hit more than compensated for the oversight in selecting nominees. He has always contended that awards are not indicative of what's the best performance of the year, although he has never declined any of the dozens of awards and honors that have been showered upon him during his brilliant career as an entertainer.

With Alan's success, his father was pushed farther into the background. Many people assumed that Bob Alda had either retired or perhaps even died. Yet Bob Alda was quite busy, working in stock, television, and nightclubs. He was happily married to a woman far more practical and less emotional than Alan's mother had been and was now the father of another son, Antony. He had plenty to keep him busy and was quite proud of Alan's accomplishments—always offering encouragement and sage advice, which Alan respected and valued. Bob's profile was that of the elder statesman settling into the comforting ease of a theatrical country squire. Alan was the young Turk, challenging and competing in the arena.

The Owl and the Pussycat was an intriguing comedy with a simple, almost taboo theme. Interracial love wasn't exactly setting new records at the marriage license bureaus. Even in the late sixties, when the play was finally being brought to the screen, it became a lily-white production. Black/white affairs (especially on film) most generally presented a theme of sadness and tragedy, or as some minor triumph over white aggression. So it had been all the more a gamble to spend money on such a Broadway production. Even the backers had some reservations, since only seventy-five thousand dollars was advanced for the production—a very small budget for any Broadway show. It was a long shot that paid off handsomely to those angels who dared to be different.

There can be very little doubt that Alan's feeling for people, and who they are deep down inside, had much to do with Phil Rose selecting him for the role and for his ability to carry off the theme of the play. One must bear in mind that this show came into being just a few months after the city of Birmingham, Alabama, had endured a long hot summer of racial riots and tensions in 1963, and even northern liberals became more cautious than they had been in the past.

None of that interfered with Alan's joy. He was a star. Acting is always somewhat of a struggle from one assignment to the next. He knew that even established actors, who turn down scripts on a daily basis, understand that stardom is precarious. He had been passed over in the Tony nominations for his performance in *Fair Game for Lovers*, but not totally ignored. He did receive a Theater World Award, which merited a prominent position on the family mantel in Leonia. It was the year in which Broadway was overrun with smash hits: *Hello Dolly!*, *Fiddler on the Roof* (both of which won Tonys and Drama Critics Circle awards), *Funny Girl* (catapulting Barbra Streisand—the future star of the film version of *The Owl and the Pussycat*—into orbit), and *The Subject Was Roses* (the Frank Gilroy masterpiece that, although a slow starter, ended up with the Pulitzer Prize, Drama Critics Circle awards plus a Tony). Alan had never before been a peer in such elite company.

Although he wasn't bowing at the podium for statuettes or making acceptance speeches, he must surely have been walking on air down the main stem each evening after listening to sell-out audiences cheer his booksy interpretation of an intellectual totally out of his element. Alan got the girl and the theatergoers had Alan. It was a fait accompli.

He must have had some pangs of déjà vu when, some years later, Hollywood got around to making a movie of *The Owl and the Pussycat*, completely ignoring the Broadway stars. Also, the film version was hardly recognizable as the same story from Bill Manhoffs original play. Alan's lessons in the humanities were getting tougher all the time. His father already knew the way Hollywood could rearrange a hit Broadway show into a film travesty of the original thing. He could empathize with his son. With Alan, the feeling probably went deeper. To him, it was more evidence of the injustices hurled at minorities.

Still, life must go on. Charity must begin at home. Alan's financial responsibilities to his family were growing. The children were starting to go to school, which meant more expense. As always, Arlene as a mother and homemaker was unequaled. If she felt any neglect as Alan pursued his own career, she did not voice it; whatever Alan wanted was fine with her. She was very busy with the everyday problems of little girls, marketing, cleaning, and meal planning for a family that was often missing its head at dinnertime. Alan spent more time in New York out of sheer obligation than he would have liked to, but he grew up in a show business family and Arlene had been in the business herself as a musician, so there was a tremendous amount of understanding between the two. This more than likely contributed to their survival as a family during those early years of seeking career and trying to bring up three daughters so close in age, each with individual demands and sensitivities. That they survived at all is testimony to a great love and understanding and allowing each other mutual space—although Alan had the better of the deal and would have for some years to come. Arlene's desires and plans would simply be put into abeyance until a more opportune time.

Between Broadway assignments, Alan worked at whatever he could find in television, mostly guest shots on the current season's sustaining series. It was not his preference. For Alan, the run of the play represented a family situation, just as "M*A*S*H" became his family away from home for so many years. Doing guest shots was like being a traveling salesman. He met new people the first time around and if he got a second appearance, then he might as well have been Avon calling or the Fuller Brush man coming back with a refill order of the same product. That was not how he enjoyed plying his craft. New dressing rooms, often shared with strangers, were uncomfortable. He had to take everything he needed to be comfortable along with him on each and every set. On a Broadway show or regular television series—even during the filming of a motion picture—some things have a sort of permanency, even if it is just a long version of temporary. Still, every appearance and every press notice was a plus.

As a distraction, Alan could be found working on or around his home in New Jersey. He never wanted to be one of those actors who needed to have everything done by an "expert." There was a part of the man that said, "I am just a simple man, the average Joe who has a few beers with the boys at the corner bar and comes home to his family ready to be a regular guy on the block." Alda's personal habits over the years seem to point toward a split personality. He has an innate need to be loved and applauded by total strangers, to be loved and worshiped for his acting ability. On the other hand, he has an equally intense desire to be anonymous, a part of a local community into which he can simply blend as a small entity within the whole. Doing a juggling act with TNT and nitroglycerin would be simpler to accomplish. Yet, Alan walks that tightrope and juggles the known and the unknown with aplomb.

He developed and espoused any number of philosophical witticisms during the run of *The Owl and the Pussycat*. He came to believe more in himself. "Of course I believe you have to take care of yourself," he said. "You can't just sit back and wait." He believed, however, in planning. "You have to know what it is you want. If you know that, then it will come to you." He also emphasized that the fulfillment of such a dream took a lot of hard work. He denied that patience was a passive folly. "It simply implies a self-assurance that inspires one to take all those little steps that lead to success." He never saw himself as a hero type, and when other leading men were posing before mirrors and seeing their favorite plastic surgeons to get that certain look that has always been expected of leading men, Alan was happy that he did not fit the mold. He considered it an advantage, which opened doors that otherwise would have been closed. "It has helped me get parts with more depth and meaning," he said. "Certainly there have been some frustrations because I didn't fit the mold, but I've managed to keep everything in perspective." He credits that perspective with helping him have a full-time family life as well as a career. He makes it sound like there are really two Alan Aldas—and maybe there are.

He was able to laugh at Arlene's predicaments, and presumably she laughed with him. Reflecting on his life in New York before taking up residence in New Jersey, he could smile. "I remember how close the girls were and Arlene had to attach a rope to Eve's tricycle, which was knotted to the carriage handle, so she could pull her up the hill. Looking back, I wonder how we did it." He allows that he was young and really didn't have any doubts about his or Arlene's abilities to bring off anything they set out to do.

He never fooled himself, however. Many of his contemporaries had to abandon their aspirations because of low income—or worse, no income. "They're very talented people, but they have to support their families," he reasoned. "I know how lucky I am."

As perspective, he had his own personal critique of his costar in *The Owl and the Pussycat*, which often surfaced during the play's Broadway run. "Playing opposite Diana requires no psychological, no technical, adjustments of any kind. The only thing I carry onstage is my own feelings about her, which is that she is a person." He was not amused that some people spoke of her as "the big step forward" being cast in a starring role opposite a white male lead. "Why not?" he asked. "What kind of step are they talking about? I perhaps shouldn't be too critical, though. I guess it is *some* kind of a step, even if only sideways." Alan understated the event. It was a first on Broadway—a black leading lady.

Alan's political and social conscience began to jell into the buds of what would be his full-bloom attacks in later years on bad politicians and social injustice. He had been attending benefit performances along with other celebrities and interested parties for causes he espoused or supported. "I will speak out," he said, "for some of the things I care about, like civil rights and pacifism." He was selective in his choices, however. "I can't go everywhere I'm invited and I don't try to do that. I go where the issue is important to me." He strongly defended the right of actors to speak out on issues, as he does today. "Why shouldn't they speak out if they feel strongly about an issue? They're citizens. Other citizens speak out, so I think we have that same right if we feel like doing it." He did worry that actors might be misused, but doubted that people took everything they said as absolute fact. "I don't think they even buy soap for that reason. My motives are really uncomplicated. I would like to see others have their fair share of the good things, too."

The activist in Alda was being nurtured and tempered. He was in the right industry to hear and see all sides of any issue. The entertainment industry has always represented a broad spectrum of political and human rights issues, both left and right. As a child he had been taunted and tormented by bullies who considered him some kind of a freak because he would rather tell jokes or clown than fight. He was merely applying those experiences to his adult rationalization of conditions and finding that strength misapplied was even less tolerable than weakness.

CHAPTER 7

Alan speaks a lot about the rights of women, but during the halcyon days of his rise to fame and fortune, he often practiced the very rituals in marriage and family that he condemns now. Arlene Alda's feelings ran the gamut from elation when she had Alan at home for a day and he could take over the girls and allow her a breathing spell to total frustration when she felt that instead of two adults in the household, there was only one. Trying to remember just who she was and her own importance in the scheme of their life often nettled Arlene. As the girls grew older and needed her less, it became time for her to think at least a bit about what she wanted for herself as well as for the family. Children grow up and have interests of their own. Alan would always have acting, to which he would add writing and directing, as the mainstay of his life. He was in the world where everything happened. Arlene fought the battle on all fronts to ensure that she did not become just another nagging housewife bemoaning all the drudgeries that befall the woman who either chooses or is forced into a career of homemaking rather than becoming a woman in the world outside the home.

Arlene Alda was not just any woman. She was a highly competent, extremely intelligent, well-educated, and accomplished lady of the arts. She had musical abilities that would have assured her a seat with any symphony orchestra in the country. Other talents lurked beneath the surface, such as photography, which she later studied and became quite professional at. As she waited for her turn in the limelight, the pressure of mothering would begin to ease and her time in the sun would eventually come. But during the sixties, it was Alan's turn at bat. He played every inning in every theatrical game in which he became involved. He was no Sammy Glick, but something motivated Alda like an inner itch that cannot be scratched but provokes one to action.

Barbara Harris, like Alan, was an alumni of *Compass*, which was reformed under the name of *Second City*. That group was responsible for many notables of today being launched into show business careers, including Alan Arkin and the multi-talented Mike Nichols and Elaine May. Barbara was a seasoned Broadway actress by the time she and Alan were coupled in *The Apple Tree*, having appeared in the off-Broadway smash *Oh Dad, Poor Dad, Mama's Hung You in the Closet and I'm Feelin' So Sad*, which had a successful, year-long run and won for her the Vernon Price Award. She later appeared in *On a Clear Day You Can See Forever* (1965), just prior to being cast in *The Apple Tree*.

Mike Nichols would direct *The Apple Tree*, so it was a matter of old friends getting together once again. Alan loved the comforts of familiarity—the same dressing room, the same theaters, and the same cast and crew, which emerged as one of the more enjoyable (for him) aspects of the ten seasons accorded "M*A*S*H" on television. The chemistry of these friendly actors clicked from the beginning and none had the slightest reservation about the success of the play, which for Alan presented the opportunity to do multiple characterizations every evening. *The Apple Tree* was considered a Broadway "first," just as *The Owl and the Pussycat* had been with its interracial theme. Jerry Brock and Sheldon Harnick wrote the score, considered the liveliest and most original of the year, and also contributed the fast-paced book. It was their first attempt at writing a libretto for Broadway. *The Apple Tree*, a trilogy based on Mark Twain's short story, "The Diary of Adam and Eve," Frank R. Stockton's "The Lady or the Tiger?" and Jules Feiffer's "Passionella," a cartoon episode, was three musicals for the price of one ($9.90 for orchestra seats).

One act has Adam and Eve discovering the world, another was set in Hollywood, with all its glitter, and the third explores unadulterated green-eyed jealousy. It was an evening of comedy, the likes of which had not been seen on Broadway boards in many years. It was a tour de force for Alan, and he romped through it with no small amount of glee, changing character at will to the running thread of Barbara's Eve. The show boasted twenty-four musical numbers, seven of which were sung by Alan (which proved that his father was not the only member of the family who could bring off a Broadway musical).

Larry Blyden, as narrator, was as acid-tongued as Vincent Price on his best day, and between him and Director Nichols there was never a moment that was not pointed and meaningful. Tony Walton's costumes ran from blah to high camp and added much zest to the pace of the three-acter. The show, produced by Stuart Ostrow, opened at the Shubert Theater on October 18, 1966. Although the play ran on, Alan was replaced by Ken Kercheval on March 27, 1967. One month later, Hal Holbrook took over the male lead. Alda returned on July 3 and remained until the play closed.

For his performance in *The Apple Tree*, Alan was again nominated for a Tony. The competition was heavy.

Cabaret, the biggest musical production of the year, received most plaudits and carried off most of the awards that year. Once again his female counterpart would take center stage. Barbara Harris won for best actress in a musical, and veteran screen and stage actor Robert Preston took the award for best male in a musical for his performance in another hit, *I Do, I Do*. It was beginning to look as if Alan could only win if he had no competition, which might offer no small amount of discouragement to him, despite his protestations against actors competing against one another for honors.

It was possibly during this period in his career that he first began to be genuinely evasive during interviews. He seemed to enjoy playing a cat-and-mouse game by the tactic of questioning the questioner when asked something specific about his couch sessions. When asked if he'd ever been in analysis, he ducked the yes-or-no response by suggesting the question was too personal. Still, he would mention having had other ailments in his life such as athlete's foot or high blood pressure. He finally did admit to "seeing someone about a particular problem at the time" but was and still is extremely evasive about any kind of contact with psychological counseling. He once indicated that mental illness was not accepted in our society, so discussing it would only be a negative force rather than a positive one. Alda seems often to overstress the positive nature of his life in what might be construed as a fear of not being totally perfect at all times.

Any number of writers who have interviewed him come away with the feeling that they have had an hour session with nothing to show for it. He is cleverly evasive and yet (in spite of his tendency to belabor the issue of privacy as a person) in any given year a little research will reveal that he tends to give dozens of interviews, especially when he is pushing some particular project.

On the flip side, it is only recently that his wife Arlene has spoken out. Rumors prevailed for years around Hollywood that his father absolutely forbade Alan's mother from speaking to the press. If true, perhaps that is why she is so reclusive today. Robert's current wife, Flora, also stays very much in the background. Arlene is made of sterner stuff, obviously, and now says what she wants when she wants. For many years, however, she never said much of anything—sort of an invisible presence in the background of Alan's life and career.

During one interview, Alan pretty much expressed the philosophy that he has adopted toward the press, except when he needs them to promote a project, when he explained why he wouldn't discuss his therapy sessions, declaring that the answer to the question was an emphatic "no!" but also that it was too personal. His final comment revealed what many people have come to call Alan Alda's manipulation complex. He said, "I want to prevent you from asking other people these questions, although that's their problem."

It is not difficult to see that Alan Alda wears his nerve network near the surface. He appears to have a somewhat perverse fear of anybody discovering what's behind the public facade—the genuine man beneath the publicity and studio hype. In 1966 he was equally sensitive, but at that time his name was not linked with any real meaning to the now-failed ERA or any number of other causes to which his name lends instant fame and recognition. Consequently, failure to be the number-one actor on Broadway did not have the psychological effect that I think he suffered recently when the ERA, for which he so wholeheartedly campaigned, failed to gain sufficient states for ratification.

Alan may have hidden his disappointment with being an also-ran in the Tony race by abandoning New York and Broadway for the bright lights and familiar childhood surroundings of Hollywood sound stages. Because that's exactly what he did—packed up and moved to California. His father, on the other hand, was still quite busy in New York, appearing on Broadway in several plays, including *What Makes Sammy Run?* as well as numerous game shows, host shows, and television soap operas.

Most have probably never heard of a television series entitled "Where's Everett?" or one called "Higher and Higher" (not to be confused with Sinatra's early motion picture), but Alan starred in both of them for CBS Television. The reason they are seldom mentioned in television lore is that even after the network invested money in the production of these pilots, the series were canceled. That must have been a shock to Alan, coming off Broadway with a more-than-average modicum of success in two successive shows.

When he arrived in Hollywood and set about to see what could be done to attract attention to himself, he was not without means. Although the two pilots had failed to gain him immediate national recognition, he was not dismayed. Quite the contrary. Whatever bitter medicine that may have turned out to be, he swallowed it and began to feel better almost at once.

While still working on Broadway in *The Apple Tree*, he had managed, through his business manager, to sew up what he probably thought would propel him to stardom in motion pictures once the play was finished and he was free to pursue work in films. He was reading with great interest one of George Plimpton's books with an eye to the future.

Plimpton has made somewhat of a name for himself as a rather determined chameleon. Not unlike Alda, he has always been considered a publicity hound. His approach was more direct than Alan's, however. George is fondly referred to as "the professional's amateur," whereas Alan might be called "the amateur's professional." George, a writer, decided to become some of the things he had or would write about. In other words, he would live the life of the athletes he so often pictured in words for newspapers and sports magazines. In order to accomplish the ends he had in mind, he fought bulls with one of his literary heroes, Ernest Hemingway; boxed in a New York gymnasium with light-heavyweight champion boxer Archie Moore (managing to hang in there and still be on his feet after three rounds); and was beaten six-love in a tennis match against tennis pro Pancho Gonzales.

One of Plimpton's exploits that received a tremendous amount of publicity was playing football with the Detroit Lions. His book, *Paper Lion*, a best seller, became a well-publicized motion picture. The film's producers cast Alan as the irrepressible Plimpton. The entire project, starring an actor who knew nothing about sports playing the role of a man who was more intruder than athlete, was farcical from start to finish.

It was material with which the fan magazines and film critics could have much fun in their publications. Some personality similarities should be noted between Plimpton and Alda. Alda, seemingly adhering to a practice of privacy from the press (always stressing privacy in his private life), was doing the exact same thing—merely using a different tack. Some unremembered publicity agent once made the aside that there were two ways to get publicity: Either saturate the media with good copy about the client or saturate the media with anecdotes about the client's desire for privacy. Both seem to work equally well.

There were other similarities. Both were liberal Democrats in their political philosophy; both supported minority and liberal causes. The personality of Hawkeye Pierce, Alda's role in the long-running "M*A*S*H" television series, might well have been patterned after Plimpton's "private life." Like Hawkeye, Plimpton has been known as somewhat of a ladies' man. His name has been linked with Princess Lee Radziwill, Ava Gardner, Candice Bergen, the late Jean Seberg, and Jane Fonda, to name but a few. Hawkeye would feel very comfortable in such company. George Plimpton was once referred to as "the last of the great bachelors," which would also fit the Hawkeye Pierce image (at least in practice).

Because of these character traits (both on and off the screen), one can see why Alda was the ideal choice for Plimpton in *Paper Lion*. Alan didn't even know how to put on shoulder pads when the film started shooting. According to Alan, he had been summoned to New York for a meeting with the film's producer, Stuart Millar, sometime before the picture was slated to start shooting. There were the routine questions to be answered. Nobody doubted Alan's acting ability. He was a proved product on Broadway. But he had never been looked at as a film actor. The producer had seen his several television outings and was impressed with what he had seen, especially Alan's seemingly effortless manner before the cameras. That was important to this particular film—to effortlessly appear amateurish. Alan, always a perfectionist, did have that particular ability: He could make a hard job look easy.

"How good an athlete are you?" he was asked. Alan, remembering that actors only have to "act" a part, rambled on for several minutes explaining a very inept performance on his part during a touch-football game in his Leonia neighborhood. A 250-pound blocker on the opposing team caught Alan in the larynx with his arm and that night his understudy had to take his place in *The Apple Tree*.

He knew that the producer and United Artists were interested when his business manager notified him a couple of nights later that the producer would like him to report to Central Park the following Sunday to play touch football. All he had to do was *look* athletic.

Sunday was only three days away and Alan begged for a delay. When asked by his manager why he needed time, Alan winced, "Because I don't know how to play touch football!"

The following day Alan bought his first football and for the next three days he kicked, passed, and punted with and to anyone who would take the time to play with him. That included his six-year-old daughter and Arlene. Tom McCormick helped him learn the moves, and Alda also worked out with a psychiatrist neighbor, who assured him that it was most important not to worry.

In Central Park on Sunday morning, with Arlene along to supply moral support, Alan arrived for his screen test. The camera was already set up and waiting for Alan's debut as a film football player. Arlene brought along her still camera, and the budding photographer clicked off pictures as Alan ran pell-mell up and down the field. As he later retold the story, Alan slipped in the fact that on the last play—a downfield pass—he *was* that Saturday (in this case, Sunday) hero. With cameras grinding away, Alan would have us all believe that he was a real pro that particular day. The fact that nobody attempted to tackle him doesn't play into the tale—but who'll know about that next year?

The real test came, however, when it was arranged to see what else he could do. *Would he please arrange to be at Yankee Stadium where the New York Giants were working out?* That afternoon's practice stretched into two weeks, and Alan was still trying to make his running pattern appear to be that of a graceful swan instead of the ugly duckling. He was working harder than he had ever worked onstage or in a film. He gained a genuine respect for the athlete he had declined to emulate as a young man. Millar took Alan to Detroit to watch the Lions play. Alan enjoyed the game. It was in the dressing room after the game that he began to feel apprehensive. Maybe the offer to play Clyde Beatty, the lion tamer, in a film was still open. At least *those* lions would be somewhat domesticated; the Detroit Lions were not. His introduction to Alex Karras, Jim Gibbons, and John Gordy of the gridiron Lions was ambivalent. If there was any awe, it was all on Alan's side. Alan's recollections of being young and pushed around by the bigger guys came back as the professional players had a field day at his expense. With the playing season over, Alan and his newfound "companions" packed their gear and flew down to Boca Raton, Florida, where the film was to be shot on location.

George Plimpton showed up in the capacity of technical adviser and consultant on the picture. He had a camaraderie with the team that Alan couldn't precisely comprehend. Plimpton was an athlete of sorts and understood the language of the athlete. The nearest Alan had come to locker-room jargon was dirty tennis socks. George was one of the boys. If George's appearance bothered Alan, he tried to shrug it off, listening to Plimpton's stories about the exploits off field with the players. Alan had not enjoyed such a close relationship, usually going home for the night when shooting was finished for the day.

Even the word games the players indulged in to pass the time in the locker room were over Alan's head—or perhaps beneath it. They usually ended up in anger, and occasionally a few bruises were bandied about—all in the spirit of athletic fun.

The players' snickers at Alan's attempts to be a football player subsided after some weeks. He wasn't good, but he was trying, and working hard to get into shape is close to every professional athlete's heart. If you aren't in shape, you don't play. Alan was probably in better physical shape than he'd ever been in his life.

Alan swears that he did his own stunts without a double, but I find it difficult to understand why any director—in this case, Alex March—would jeopardize a multimillion-dollar production in order to permit his star the luxury of being squashed by the front line of the Detroit Lions. A feature article, by-lined by Alan Alda, says that Roger Brown crushed his rib cage, McCord and McCambridge plowed in right behind, and Alex Karras—a genuine giant—"drilled his cleats into my ankle." According to Alan, there was a speck of lint on the camera lens and he repeated the scene again. Alan garnered more publicity for that one. Arlene was on hand throughout the filming, properly recording Alan's exploits with her still camera.

Despite Plimpton's reputation, the Detroit Lions as a supporting cast, *and* doing his own stunt work, Alan was unable to become as superstar through his performance in *Paper Lion*. There simply wasn't anything that outstanding about the film.

CHAPTER 8

While Alan was struggling to become a movie star, his father was applying himself in several directions. He appeared in Broadway productions, hosted television shows, made movies (usually in supporting roles), and found that he adapted quite well to daytime soap operas, playing the character of Jason Ferris, for instance, in both "Love of Life" and "The Secret Storm" (CBS), which prepared him for his sustaining role today on the daytime serial, "Days of Our Lives."

Alan did his share of guest-stinting on the various television panel shows. He was by now considered more a personality than an established star, although he'd been active in his career for over ten years. When he appeared on the popular television show "What's My Line?" Alan was dubbed "an owl." Gil Fates, in his book *What's My Line?* which is a history of that show, described owls in the following paragraph:

Owls stumped the panel simply because the panelists didn't know they existed. How can you identify a person you never saw or even heard of? And Mystery Guest owls exhibited remarkably similar behavior. They squeaked and squawked outrageously in a desperate effort to convince the audience that it was the vocal disguise rather than the anonymity that had the panel bamboozled. In truth their natural voices would have had precisely the same effect, namely none.

The regular panelists soon became familiar with Alan, as he frequently became part of the show as a guest panelist rather than a mystery guest. His wit, when properly applied, was considered a plus on what might otherwise be a mundane segment of the show. Gil Fates was the show's producer and it was his feeling that "What's My Line?" was responsible for the "discovery" of Alan Alda along with several of today's " names" in show business—and he may well have been correct in that assumption. "What's My Line?" was an extremely popular show that made the names of regular panelists Arlene Francis, Bennett Cerf, Dorothy Kilgallen, and moderator John Daly household words.

Alan's career was like a Yo-Yo at this point. He was neither a major star nor supporting actor. He took whatever roles were offered (if his track record for that time and place are carefully scrutinized) as though he expected a lucky break or a meaty role to project him to stardom overnight. There can be very little doubt that the late sixties and early seventies were the doldrums of his career. His television appearances were sporadic and merely that—appearances. Also, he should have been able to see the writing on the wall. Motion-picture acting was not doing much more than keeping his name in the media from time to time with so-so or inadequate reviews.

In 1969 he made a film for John Frankenheimer, prior to Frankenheimer's critical success, *The Fixer*. The film was set in the South Pacific. The rather innocuous plot involved three sailors who were marooned on an island, totally removed from World War II. The essence of the story was how their life was actually compared to the propaganda intercuts from old World War II newsreels; for instance, Bess Truman tries desperately to launch a ship while unable to break the bottle of champagne. Probably the only reason the picture had been made was to focus in on the Vietnam War, which had stirred up so much national emotion, since the film really ridiculed war as a treacherous game that sensible and sane people did not play. It is ironic, however, that he would later become a television superstar in a series that also, in spite of the bloody nature of "M*A*S*H," would poke holes in the feasibility of man fighting man on the battlefield.

Critics were not cruel, nor were they kind, to this unextraordinary film tided *The Extraordinary Seaman*, which also starred Faye Dunaway and David Niven. The film was not released for over a year after its completion because the studio wasn't sure of American theatergoers' reaction to the satiric use of World War II propaganda film as inserts. Thousands of American young men were dying and being maimed in what would turn out to be a useless war in Vietnam. The timing of this picture's finish had everything to do with the apprehensions about its release. *The Fixer*, made after *The Extraordinary Seaman*, was released first. Having been such a depressing film, it probably contributed to the box office of *Seaman* (as meager as it was)—a comedy—even if the jokes and routines were repetitive and predictable.

Seaman, in spite of anything else that might be said for or against it, was vintage Alan Alda humor. His niche in fame will always be garlanded with military spoofs. MGM, the studio that produced *The Extraordinary Seaman*, did not ask Alan to sign a long-term contract, although, for reasons known only to themselves, they did star him in another nothing picture immediately afterward.

Not only were *The Extraordinary Seaman* as well as *The Moonshine War* (the second film) less than critical successes, they were both disasters at the box office. It was not dissimilar to sending out two ships over uncharted courses, the second following the sinking of the first. Alan almost never discusses either of these films in public if he can avoid it. *Seaman* had been a spoof (or an attempted one) of the military. From that he went into *The Moonshine War*, a melodrama set in the depression. The results were financially and critically a rerun of Pearl Harbor. Its theatrical exhibition life was short, and MGM did not go for strike three.

It might be reasoned that even if Alan was not critically accepted as a genius and fans were not lining up, he was working and earning more money than he ever had before. Supporting a wife and three daughters was now an easier task, and the days of side-line employment were something to reminisce about over good wine rather than hassle with between auditions and casting calls. For better or worse, he was in Hollywood and he had already made more motion pictures than his father had during a longer tenure in Tinseltown.

Chauvinistic, macho, or feminist—it is difficult to label Alda. He is like a crawfish. Just when you think you have him in your hands, with one quick swoosh he is gone. He has practiced elusiveness with the tenacity of Howard Hughes, and still, like Hughes, he has always known how to attract the media when he needs it. In that sense his ability to manipulate is featured and can be justly labeled as exerting a certain type of control over the press.

During all those years in the sixties, when he was making one bomb after another in Hollywood, he kept his wife and children completely away from the glittering life of a Hollywood celebrity. Alone and loose in a town where beautiful girls abound and more than outnumber males, his opportunities to womanize were abundant. Yet there was never the slightest hint that Alan partook or was even tempted. Outside his family, his pursuits always seemed to be toward his work. That is a traditional and admirable trait in a man—one not often found in famous people and certainly not among today's celebrities, for whom bed-hopping is as popular as reading the daily Hollywood trade journals.

During this hectic period of bad films, Arlene Alda must have played not only the role of wife and companion, but also a confidante to the man who came home on weekends bearing frustrations and anger with the industry that was not taking him seriously as an actor, with the media that did not credit his work in films as important.

Arlene Alda probably hit it squarely on the button when she said that her husband was an actor, but what he really wanted to be was a writer. No longer the chubby little boy that other kids poked fun at, the residual effects of that childhood pain probably recurred numerous times when the big boys in the media clobbered him with their big stick—the film critique.

Although somewhat of a loner all of his life, he did make friends—people like Rita Moreno, with whom he did the road company production of his New York success, *The Owl and the Pussycat* His friends have profited from their association with him. Rita Moreno is a prime example of Alan's wanting people he was comfortable with working with him on pictures. Later on, when he made *The Four Seasons*, Rita's friendship came to the fore when she was awarded a starring role in the film.

Alan continued making inroads into the inner palaces of glamour and glitter. Following a dismal series of films, he refocused and tried again with a picture for Cinerama in 1970 called *Jenny* in which his costar was the popular television star of "That Girl," Mario Thomas. Here again was an instance of forming a lifelong friendly alliance. Mario Thomas considers Alan one of her very best friends and attests to his loyalty and warmth. Thomas, who during the run of her long-time series in the late sixties was at times considered difficult to work with by some of her crew and co-workers, has always been a private person and probably learned from her father's exposure over the years that stars need to steal all of the time they can legitimately get away with. That would cause her to have empathy for Alda's stance on privacy. The need for privacy may have been the root of those complaints against her, and to some degree that may apply in Alan's case also.

Thomas had a lot at stake in *Jenny*. After five years on a top-rated television series, this would be her first motion picture for the wide screen, and ever the meticulous perfectionist, she wanted it to be letter-perfect. She was keenly aware (again because of her father's career) that television stars rarely make the transition from the little screen in the living room to movie theaters. That the film did not quite come off as expected is not to discredit the acting in this instance. It was a thinly contrived plot that cast Miss Thomas as a naive, sweetly melancholy doll who never bothers with birth control because it has never really occurred to her that she could get pregnant. She predictably does get with child, fathered by a married man whose happy home she refuses to break up. Consequently, she suppresses the facts of life from her seducer. She's not too dumb to know that her offspring will need a father, so she zeroes in on Alan Alda, an avowed draft dodger, who picks her for the patsy of the year who will, by giving him a marriage of convenience, conveniently keep him out of the army. The male role was subservient to the wronged woman. Although the story of wronged girl had been successfully brought to the screen many, many times, *Jenny* was not to be in the ranks of the memorable ones, despite the prestige of inaugurating the opening of Avco-Embassy's newest theater in Beverly Hills.

Although *Jenny* was nominated for no awards, it did at least break even at the box office, and for once Alan was identified with a film that did not lose money in the theaters. It is said that money begets money, and in no other place is that a more ringing statement than in Hollywood.

Coming off a picture with a costar who was the successful daughter of a successful father was the best of timing for Alan. It brought about a studio association that would serve him well in the years to come and eventually bring him to the stature of a Johnny Carson or Frank Sinatra in the sense of "juice" or "clout," the two most used expressions in the film industry for power.

Quinn Martin Productions was preparing to do a film for Twentieth Century-Fox called *The Mephisto Waltz.* The film, to be directed by Paul Wendkos, was based on the novel of the same name by Fred Mustard Stewart—an occult-oriented tome. The book was timely for filming, coming on the heels of *Rosemary's Baby*, which was a trend-setter in occult films. *The Mephisto Waltz,* from a critical point of view, was no more than a sleazy attempt to capitalize on the popularity and audience appeal of *Rosemary's Baby.* One critic went so far as to say it should have been called "Rosemary's Grandchild." The comment was not made to flatter the film. If the picture was mediocre, the cast was not. In addition to Alan, it also boasted Jacqueline Bisset, Barbara Parkins of "Peyton Place" fame, Bradford Dillman, and William Windom.

Alda's role was that of an unsuccessful concert pianist who, with his wife (played by Bisset), lives in a small cottage above the Sunset

Strip in the Hollywood Hills. Bisset manages a small boutique that supports the duo along with their nine-year-old daughter Abby.

Granted an audition with the world's greatest pianist, Duncan Ely (played in true Prussian style by Curt Jurgens), Alda receives a somewhat icy reception until the great master discovers that Alda has "Rachmaninoff hands." After numerous deaths and ink dots on foreheads, Alda through black magic inherits the face and talents of the pianist and finds himself in the end saddled with Ely's daughter Roxanne, who just happens to wear Shalimar perfume, the favorite of his now-deceased wife. It was the kind of film most stars make in the sunset of their career, not the ascent. It certainly came as no surprise that *Rosemary's Baby* would be duplicated in various forms. It is an old tried and true custom of Hollywood film-makers. Every producer in Los Angeles suddenly has a "new idea," which found its roots in the success of another film. We have recently seen that phenomena reassert itself following *Star Wars*. Why Alan, if he was serious about a career, ever undertook any of these pictures in light of his present sense of selectivity is an enigma. Perhaps one explanation is that he would do anything, as I've pointed out earlier, in order to maintain a public profile. Alan Alda is not an illiterate. A man aspiring to an eventual career as a writer must have read the script before he consented to do the picture.

Many critics tore the picture apart with vulture sharp talons:

Joseph Gelmis, *Newsday*: "Son of Rosemary's Baby."

Anitra Earle, *San Francisco Chronicle*: "For sheer horror, a suburban housewife in stretch pants beats it any day."

William Wolf, *Cue* magazine: "Ludicrous solemnity ... a script that collapses hopelessly ... director Paul Wendkos is so intent on making his film seem stylish that everything comes out mumbo-jumbo instead of shocking."

Charles Champlin, *Los Angeles Times*: "Despite glossy production values and a lot of arty, jiggery-pokery photography which seems to be doing more than it really is, *The Mephisto Waltz* makes you shudder only in the sense that a yawn does."

Judith Crist: "The problem arises in the Alan Alda character. A sexually sluggish and complacent husband, he is definitely enlivened if not improved by the acquisition of Curt Jurgens' soul... there are no operations and no closed-circuit television privileges and it all happens so invisibly that you're not quite sure at the end whose soul is where."

While filming *The Mephisto Waltz*, Alan became friendly with Glenn Ford's son, Peter, a dialogue coach on the film. They spent long hours playing word games and Peter recalls that Alan was an expert. "There was one word," Peter says, "that Alan didn't recognize and it drove him right up the wall until he finally looked it up." He thought Peter had made the word up. Several years later, when Peter's wife, Lynda—an actress—was working on a segment of "M*A*S*H," she encountered Alda by a water fountain on the Fox lot and casually mentioned the word. Alan, with a memory like a steel trap, raised his head from the fountain, grinned, and said, "How's Peter these days?"

Alan was dabbling in automatic writing at that time and discussed it quite often with Peter. He also gave the subject some mileage during an interview with columnist/ author Joyce Haber during a round of meetings with the press to promote the film. "I've always been interested in the occult," he said, "but not Satanism [the theme of *The Mephisto Waltz*]. I really don't want to get mixed up with Satanism."

He told Haber that his interest in the occult was part of a life-long investigation into just who Alan Alda is. His interest probably stemmed from a part-time job he had in New York while struggling to find work as an actor. One of his many part-time occupations was that of guinea pig to a psychiatrist in the field of hypnosis. "The experience was invaluable," he assured her. "It's probably dangerous to let your mind go—to use ESP, as many people do, like a toy, to let children play with a Ouija board, or to try automatic writing. These are ways to let yourself go to whatever force wants to take over your brain at the time."

Alda has also read most or all of the Edgar Cayce books on clairvoyance and is knowledgeable on the subject. "In automatic writing," he advises, "you let yourself go in the hope that your hand will write by itself. People who have done this have found that their hands have written in foreign languages that they themselves can't speak."

Alan Alda is also interested in hypnosis. "A light trance," he says, "gives you the best of both possible worlds. It puts you on the right threshold, giving the freedom of being lost, yet having the power to control." He compares it with the moments preceding sleep. "It's the state all those kids are trying to attain with all the junk they're stuffing into their systems."

This all transpired during the late summer and early fall of 1970, prior to his national prominence in "M*A*S*H." It is, so far as I can ascertain, the beginning of what some have called "the opinionated Alan Alda."

Probably the most revealing aspect that remains in one's mind from that interview was an observation from Ms. Haber. Alan Alda, she summarizes, "clearly believes in chauvinism." Alda adds, "I can't listen to a whole evening of anecdotes" and "I'm not interested in Toledo." About a month after the Haber interview appeared in the *Los Angeles Times*, Alan was asked to say something original about Hollywood. He said, "I don't have anything original to say about what happened to Hollywood." Then, he went on to dispense the opinion that Hollywood was too trendy, that the trends used to be musicals. If boxing movies are popular, then the producers will give us a run on boxing films (which was very prophetic, since we've seen the *Rocky* syndrome). Also, "I think we're all suffering from bad bets. It's bad gambling—bad speculation. We always have suffered from bad art—from nonart—in movies."

Alan, in a sense, also predicted what he was expecting from himself in the future. He said, "It may be that this decline, if it leads to more personal movies being made because they have to be made on a smaller budget, personal movies made on one man's individual genius or inspiration rather than a committee's lack of inspiration and basing the decisions on what's worked before ... because if you are more personal about an artistic product you will be more creative."

Alda's thinking and philosophy have also been influenced by author Carlos Castaneda, whose controversial books have all been best sellers, especially in the United States. In his book *The Teachings of Don Juan*, Castaneda says, "Never take a path that has no heart in it." Alan's response to that line is, "You can't lose if your heart is in your work, but you can't win if your heart is not in it." While Alan philosophized about Hollywood and acting, he did not abandon his family relationships. During his stay in Hollywood, making one film after another, he maintained a small apartment near the Westwood campus of UCLA, which brought him in closer focus to his home in Leonia, New Jersey, which was also a college town, although the population of the large Westwood campus was easily five times that of the entire city of Leonia.

When he went back to New Jersey on weekends or during breaks in shooting, he resumed the active role of suburban father. He helped out with the housework. He loves to cook and sometimes does the ironing, although forthrightly stating that he enjoys ironing, "only if I don't have to do it." He would also take an active hand in the lives of his three young daughters. He was always afraid they would grow up as "Hollywood brats" if he and Arlene did not bend over backward to assure that they didn't. Consequently, both parents endeavored to give more of themselves to their offspring than money and material possessions. Expensive cars (when they were old enough to have them) were out of the question, although all three girls were gifted with sensible automobiles when the time was right.

While Arlene and Alan mixed Alan's West Coast career in the movies with old-fashioned turn-of-the-century family standards, Alan's father was again walking the boards on Broadway in a revival of Ben Hecht and Charles MacArthur's great play, *The Front Page*. Alan's mother had disappeared from the public eye completely and during interviews Alan either sidetracked any in- depth conversation about her or reporters tactfully did not ask, knowing that he preferred not to discuss her private life, since she no longer was even in the shadow of celebrity. Arlene was now the woman behind the man, not Alan's mother.

CHAPTER 9

On February 4, 1972, *The New CBS Friday Night Movies* did something quite different from what had ever been done before on television. With the full cooperation of the Utah Department of Corrections they had shot a feature-length film on location at the Utah State Prison, *The Glass House,* based on Truman Capote's scathing attack on the American system of prisons and their treatment of their charges. The lucky stars of this unusually frank and dynamic film were Vic Morrow, Billy Dee Williams, Dean Jagger, and Alan Alda. Dean Jagger did not need any boost to his long career, but Morrow, Williams, and Alda owe much to their appearance in *The Glass House.*

The film, several years before our youngsters were shocked into reality by *Scared Straight,* let the American television viewer see what prisons are really like—the brutal killings, beatings by guards, snitches, interracial friction, and homosexuality. It was a rare view from the comfortable living rooms across the country. Alan played Jonathan Paige, an otherwise solid citizen who is convicted of manslaughter and sentenced to prison. What we really see is the "modern" prison through the eyes of this good citizen, who is trapped by our archaic methods of dealing with the products of a society who find themselves behind locked gates and bars of a state penitentiary.

It would prove to be Alan's greatest moment on film and would guarantee him the instant recognition all around the country that he had been unable to secure previously, in spite of much critical acclaim on Broadway. *The Glass Home* had its share of production problems, not the least of which was in the writing of the teleplay. The producers, Bob Christiansen and Rick Rosenberg, along with director Tom Gries, had originally signed Truman Capote to write the screenplay from his own story. Problems quickly ensued. Capote was replaced by a young screenwriter at the last minute. The assignment was turned over to Tracy Keenan Wynn (great-grandson of matinee idol Frank Keenan, grandson of famed comedian Ed Wynn, and the son of Hollywood stalwart Keenan Wynn), who had recently won an Emmy for his first screenplay, *Tribes*.

Wynn took one look at Capote's screenplay and tossed it in the wastebasket. "I didn't think Capote's screenplay was a good one, so I started right from scratch," he said. "I finished a new first draft in less than two weeks." His final script was completed on location at the Utah State Prison in Salt Lake City while Gries was already shooting the film.

Wynn and Alda had great rapport. Both were concerned about social issues and both wanted an iron curtain drawn between their private and public lives. Wynn remembers that the convicts confined to the Utah State Prison were of immense help in writing the script. "I had as a technical director an ex-con who spent twelve years in San Quentin for murder. I also circulated about the prison talking with the convicts, often right in their cells, the coffee room, and wherever I might run into them."

He circulated the completed script among the three hundred or so inmates who were interested in reading it for accuracy.

"Many of them came in with comments and criticisms," Wynn says, "which was of tremendous help in creating the realism we were interested in putting on the screen." At night, back in their hotel, Wynn discussed his day's writing with the actors, who were always in conversation with the prisoners, trying to emulate on the screen the lives of men they hoped never to duplicate away from the cameras.

Alan considered Utah State Prison one of the more liberal penal institutions in the country but found it depressing to see institutional confinement firsthand. He was appalled that the state's charges were given no opportunity to learn a meaningful trade and that there was no therapy available for them. "Their so-called rehabilitation program is useless and they're desperate for help." He would like to have seen the average American citizen spend some time there so that people on the outside would see how their money was being wasted on ineffective programs.

Wynn said, "By the time we finished up there, I'd lost my sense of humor."

Alda was storing away data in his mental files of social injustice. He was very much in agreement with Tracy Wynn, who wrote that "The Glass House is as much a documentary as it is fabricated drama.... Paradoxically, both the inmates and the guards must deal with the same issues simultaneously, since inside the walls of a prison everyone is equally a prisoner."

Many television executives frowned on such bare-knuckled prison life being brought into America's living rooms, which had been for so long saturated with inane sit-coms, but did not move to overly censor what had been shot at the prison before it reached the television screen.

If Alan had immediate rapport with Wynn, that was not always the case in his relationship with the director, Tom Gries, whose practical jokes were sometimes aimed at his star. Alda's discomfiture was evidenced by the coldness between the two men. Professionals, however, they brought off the production to perfection.

During the filming of The Glass House, Alan's agent sent him a script that would eventually change his life dramatically and bring a welcome relief to a public starving for comedy that did not insult the viewer's intelligence. Larry Gelbart and Gene Reynolds were preparing a new series pilot for Twentieth Century-Fox Films television division, a comedy about surgeons in the Korean War. "M*A*S*H," the projected series, would be based on the highly successful motion picture of the same name, which had starred Donald Sutherland as Hawkeye Pierce (the role being offered Alda in the series).

In the interim between the time Alan received the first series of "M*A*S*H" scripts and before he signed to do the series, he made a television movie that ABC aired on October 3, 1972. The television movie *Playmates*, which costarred Alan Alda and Doug McClure, was another step in the maturation of Alan Alda in movies. The story involved two divorced fathers and the relationship they had with their sons. It was a mature and honest film. There can be little doubt that 1970 marked the end of the old Alan Alda and the beginning of the new, which culminated in Alan's accepting the "M*A*S*H" series.

Some background is important to place "M*A*S*H" in proper perspective and to understand Alan's relationship to the series, given his devotion to pacifism and his total abhorrence of war and any kind of violence. "M*A*S*H" originated as a novel by Richard Hooker, who in private life, is Dr. H. Richard Hornberger, a surgeon and much-beloved medical doctor who lives in Waterville, Maine, on an almost isolated inlet. Dr. Hornberger is a shy man who in appearance and manner typifies the small-town family doctor in the tradition of a Norman Rockwell painting during the early forties. He appears to be light-years away in personality from his creation of the flamboyant booze-guzzling, woman-chasing Hawkeye Pierce and Trapper John McIntyre (played by Elliott Gould in the film version, which was directed by Robert Altman). Dr. Hornberger has never considered himself a writer. Authoring novels has been somewhat of a hobby for him. He never dreamed that his romance with humorous books (he has penned several since the advent of his best-selling original M*A*S*H novel) would take him to the dizzying heights it has.

Yet Dr. Hornberger *is* Hawkeye Pierce. Crabapple Cove, the rustic name given to the particular area where the doctor and his family (his wife of thirty-six years and their five children) live is a very quiet and sane spot on earth, very different from the Korea he wrote about in M*A*S*H and the sequel, a postwar effort, called M*A*S*H Goes to Maine. Hornberger's intimate friends affectionately refer to him as "Horny," a nickname reminiscent of Hawkeye Pierce's reputation for woman-chasing.

I asked Dr. Hornberger about Alan's portrayal of the Hawkeye Pierce character he created, and he said, "I have never met Mr. Alda, and I have no strong feelings one way or another about his portrayal of Hawkeye." That terse response is in keeping with the image most of us have of the word-sparing New England squire. Still, in a 1973 interview with Neil Hickey of TV Guide, he confesses to a Walter Mitty-like existence: "Hawkeye does a lot of the things I'd like to do." When asked if he likes the "M*A*S H*" television series, there is a twinkle in his eye when he responds, "I'm not going to knock anything that pays me an extra gall bladder a week for no work." Hornberger receives three hundred dollars each time a segment of "M*A*S*H" is aired. He compares that to "finding money in the street." "M*A*S H*" was based on the doctor's experience as a surgeon in Korea in 1952. As part of a group of young surgeons, many of whom were drafted right out of their internships and residencies, he endured the rigors of a field hospital with the dead and dying being brought in around the clock by helicopter or on litters. "We worked long, hard hours in makeshift operating rooms with a philosophy that said, 'Do the job well, and after that—do as you please.' We were out there in the middle of nowhere. What could they do, fire us?"

He seems to feign surprise that he was even qualified to be a doctor when the war in Korea broke out. "I had the lowest marks of any pre-med student in the class at Bowdoin College and at Cornell Medical School. A friendly chemistry teacher at Bowdoin got me into Cornell with an application that said, in effect: "This guy may be a little peculiar, but I think he's worth taking a chance on." The Hawkeye Pierce character emerges sometimes in his regular routine. "You could get a lot of people around Thayer Hospital to tell you I'm a screwball."

Although Dr. Hornberger makes the one-hundred-mile round trip from his home on the cove to Waterville several times a week, he, like Alan Alda, is strictly a man who prefers the home fires over Main Street on Saturday nights. "I never wanted to be anyplace else. I see no reason ever to go south of Portland."

One big difference between the original Hawkeye Pierce and the two men who have played him, Donald Sutherland and Alan Alda, is that Hornberger is a staunch Republican conservative and the other two are liberals with strong attachments to liberal causes.

Sutherland, like Hornberger, was totally surprised at the success of "M*A*S*H."

"We had no idea what would happen," he says in reference to the filming of the motion picture. "In fact, Elliott Gould and I thought we were in a disaster. I could see the end of my career." Of course quite the opposite was true. His career skyrocketed following the release of "M*A*S*H." Sutherland was reported to have been paid approximately $20,000 for his role in "M*A*S*H." Alan Alda has made millions from his television portrayal of Hawkeye Pierce. Sutherland says that every time he sees Alan Alda he thanks him for giving him a long-running television series. Sutherland has never publicly stated whether or not he was offered the television series, but Alda is grateful in either event.

So there was a solid premise for Hornberger's book which Robert Altman, always a controversial director, brought to the screen and Larry Gelbart and Gene Reynolds created as an institution on television. Wayne Rogers had already been signed to play the role of Trapper John when the script was sent to Alan Alda. Alda, by that time, a well-known pacifist didn't immediately jump for joy at the prospect of being some kind of war hero glorifying murder on the battlefield.

Alda said later, "My greatest concern was that the show would become a thirty-minute commercial for the Army." It was at his insistence, he says, that Gelbart guarantee that each segment of the show have inserted into it at least one operating-room sequence. Doing a comedy series about life in a mobile Army surgical hospital during the

Korean War was a touchy situation. The series would be filming while a very real war was going on in Vietnam, one that Alan Alda was totally against. There were considerations of public acceptance to be dealt with. Alan did not want to be considered pro-war. Therefore, for him to ground in heavy character roles, didn't think he would be able to do comedy. The producers convinced the casting department that they were wrong, and he was given the part, which had only half a dozen lines in the first episode, so if he flunked out it would be no big loss. He succeeded beyond anybody's expectations.

WAYNE ROGERS, by all pre-casting predictions, this handsome, almost devil-may-care personality should have been the dominating factor in "M*A*S*H," not the somewhat dour and acrid-humored, unhandsome, gangly Alda. Once asked to describe himself, Rogers cracked, "I am emotionally impulsive and think I have a large thirst for life." However, he never felt he was emotionally equipped to handle in real life the daily confrontations his television character endured. Rogers was one of the "good ol' boys"—an Alabama country kid who grew up a few miles from Birmingham and went on to Princeton University, where he graduated in 1954 with a major in history. He went into the U.S. Navy and it looked as if he would go on to make a career of the military service—until, that is, his ship was ordered into dry-dock at the Brooklyn Navy Yard and he went to a rehearsal of a play his friend was directing. He resigned his naval commission and, like Gary Burghoff, went to New York to study with Sandy Meisner. After the usual off-Broadway breaking in as an actor, he became a regular on the daytime soap opera "The Edge of Night." He went on to become a series regular, costarring with the late William Bendix in "Stagecoach West." His big movie break came in Robert Wise's *Odds Against Tomorrow.* He, more than anyone else, was probably selected for "M*A*S*H" because he was a proved product—a success—in television (plus he was good-looking and had a "Peck's bad boy" smile, sure to attract female viewers).

McLEAN STEVENSON comes from the political family with the same name. Born in Normal, Illinois, he is a graduate of Northwestern University. His cousin was Adlai E. Stevenson II—a two-time presidential candidate on the Democratic ticket. McLean worked for Adlai as his press secretary. It was the presidential hopeful who encouraged McLean to forget politics or any other pursuit and seek an acting life. He, too, studied under Sandy Meisner (and others) in New York and went on to work in several road companies of such smash Broadway hits as *Brigadoon, Music Man,* and *West Side Story.* The multitalented Stevenson was not on the unemployment rolls when he came to California. He had been financially successful as a writer and actor in both television and radio as well as on the stage. Upon his arrival in Hollywood, he snagged a costarring role with Doris Day in her hit weekly, "The Doris Day Show," and a second role on "The Tim Conway Show." It was one of those rare instances when an actor can sustain himself on two weekly shows at the same time. Gene Reynolds also produced the popular "Room 222" series, and when Doris Day and Tim Conway both left the air, Stevenson auditioned for "Room 222." He did not get the part, but Reynolds remembered him and thought enough of his ability to offer him the role in "M*A*S*H," which resulted in his being a regular on the show for three years.

LORETTA SWIT. Sally Kellerman created the role of "Hot Lips" Houlihan in Bob Altman's film version of M*A*S*H. Loretta Swit has been the only woman to portray the role in the series. She, too, came to Hollywood by way of New York, having also studied at the American Academy of Dramatic Arts and later under-studying Sandy Dennis in *Any Wednesday* on Broadway. She would later segue into the Dennis role opposite Gardner McKay, who never quite made it in Hollywood despite his highly touted physical presence, which was once compared to that of Tyrone Power.

When Loretta came to Hollywood in the late sixties, she made the "guest star" rounds of the current rash of series and was quite busy when her agent sent her in to audition for Hot Lips Houlihan. She almost didn't make it to the Fox Studios to see Gene Reynolds because of a shopping commitment. Luckily for her, the department store was near the studio and she doubled her pleasure by shopping and then dropping into the studio, not really expecting anything earthshaking to take place. The rest is history. She is one of the few actors who have been with the series from its inception.

The producers and writers of the pilot show had their own track records to contribute to the making of the long-running, highly successful series:

LARRY GELBART is one of those rare individuals considered to be "a writer's writer," "a producer's writer," and "a star's writer." He has always enjoyed tremendous popularity both in the front office and on the set. Originally from Chicago, there was never any doubt in his mind that he would be a writer. While attending Fairfax High School in West Hollywood, he set about accomplishing his goal. It is interesting that CBS Television City sprung up a few blocks down Fairfax Avenue from his alma mater and that "M*A*S*H" is one of the greatest money-makers CBS has ever screened. He wrote for the popular Fanny Brice and Danny Thomas radio shows while still a teen-ager and obtained invaluable experience (which he would later use in the writing of "M*A*S*H") writing for Armed Forces Radio Network. With a great flair for comedy writing, Larry was a stalwart upon whose shoulders it often fell to make guys like Danny Thomas, Johnny Carson, and Bob Hope (among many others) look and sound funny. He had "the knack."

He was a tireless worker, running up credits that would be the envy of writers who had been hacking away long before he arrived on the scene. His screenplays included *The Notorious Landlady* (a highly successful film that enhanced the careers of Kim Novak and Jack Lemmon) and the smash Broadway show, starring funny man Zero Mostel, *A Funny Thing Happened on the Way to the Forum*. Gelbart was already the winner of several prestigious writing awards and his type of humor was ready-made for the message-oriented "M*A*S*H."

BURT METCALFE went from acting to producing, by way of numerous behind-the-scenes positions in the film business. He was a casting director at Universal Television when Gene Reynolds, whom Metcalfe knew when they were both actors, then a producer-director, asked him to cast a film Reynolds was producing. When Reynolds decided he wanted Burt to bring his expertise to the "M*A*S*H" team, he offered him the more secure position of associate producer. Burt became known as "Mr. Fix-it" because of his ability to doctor an ailing script and make changes in dialogue to fit the character—the little everyday housekeeping chores that make everything seem easy.

GENE REYNOLDS, if there is, truly such a character as "the brains behind the scenes," is that person on "M*A*S*H" and has been since the idea for a series was conceived. When Twentieth Century-Fox decided to do a series following the smash success of the movie *M*A*S*H*, Gene Reynolds was chosen to be the producer and given leeway to select his own people both behind the cameras and on the screen. It was the carte blanche every producer strives to obtain from a studio and is rarely given. Just as he was selected by Twentieth Century-Fox because the studio felt he was the one person who could put the series together, he was equally selective in picking a cast and crew. He went to England, where Larry Gelbart was working, because he wanted Gelbart and nobody else. It was the same with Metcalfe, and each of the featured players. Had he listened to others, Alan Alda might not have played Hawkeye Pierce in the pilot because Alan, very much engrossed in *The Glass House* location shooting in Utah, held up giving a firm commitment. But Reynolds never really considered anybody else.

Gene's career began as a contract actor under the old studio star system at MGM during the strong-arm days of movie mogul Louis B. Mayer. A navy veteran from World War II, he returned to Hollywood after the war to act in movies. Unable to find permanent work, Reynolds took a job working in a Beverly Hills men's store. One day the talent chief from NBC came into the store and from the casual visit (she was impressed that he would do anything to make a living when she knew he had so much talent) came the opportunity to become a casting director. From that time on, he worked behind, not in front of, the cameras, except for a brief stint as an actor on the pilot segment of Jackie Cooper's series "Hennessy." By the time he was given the "M*A*S*H" assignment, his track record resembled a reference volume of Emmy nominations and awards. He had behind him, as a director, assignments on prime-time series around the dial: "Peter Gunn," "Hogan's Heroes," "Leave It to Beaver," "My Three Sons," "The Andy Griffith Show," and "Hennessy." He was dismissed by ABC Television as producer on the extremely popular series, "The Ghost and Mrs. Muir" because of differences of opinion. Bill Self, an executive at Fox, then handed him the "M*A*S*H" series.

Whether the producers or the studio—or even CBS—knew that "M*A*S*H" would become one of television's highest rated, longest-running shows is academic now. The point is, that closely knit group who assembled at Twentieth Century-Fox one morning and heard producer-director Gene Reynolds yell "action!" was the beginning of a new era in television programming.

CHAPTER 10

The early reviews of "M*A*S*H" were mixed. The show was immediately compared to the more sexually aggressive and bloodier film version. Alan Alda was not an instant national hero, nor did the critics write adulating reviews about the show. James Nathan of the *Chicago Tribune* said this:

It is bound to bring down the wrath of those who feel that Sunday evening television should be as pure as the driven snow. "M*A*S*H" certainly isn't that pure.

The sexual aggressiveness, though it is probably some sort of high-water mark for a television comedy series, and the funny lines tossed about by doctors who are up to their elbows in some soldier's spleen will not by themselves make "M*A*S*H" a hit.

What I think you will like is the cast, and particularly the supporting players.

He suggested that Alan Alda and Wayne Rogers were only "reasonably" successful in carrying off the roles of Hawkeye Pierce and Trapper John McIntyre. He felt the show would be popular, if at all, because of the "zany characters" played by Larry Linville and Loretta Swit, with additional kudos to McLean Stevenson and Gary Burghoff. He did not see it as a hit. "Theirs," he wrote, "is the kind of comedy situation that might wear thin after a few shows, but in the short run it is a lot of fun." He considered the pilot a "poor effort." That, however, did not bother him excessively. "The plot," he added, "seems unimportant. It is the fun of getting there, whatever silly place that might be, that promises to be the series' strong suit."

In the beginning, the producers tried to keep the television "M*A*S*H" in line with the film, so there were similarities in the makeup of the series. For instance, the exterior scenes were shot at the Twentieth Century-Fox ranch in Malibu, while the interior scenes were all shot in the big "M*A*S*H" sound stage at the Fox studios in Westwood.

"M*A*S*H" couldn't expect to compete immediately with the regular Sunday night fare against which it was slotted: ABC's "The FBI" (starring the extremely popular, low-key, no-nonsense Efrem Zimbalist, Jr.) and the NBC perennial, "The Wonderful World of Disney." CBS had for a long time made attempts to crack the eight o'clock Sunday night hold held by its rival networks to no avail. Pitting "M* A*S* H" against "The FBI" and Disney was, in a television sense, like sending an untried David out to slay not one but two Goliaths. The producers and stars of the show would have not been thought insane if they had announced commitments for other projects the following season—or even when new shows were dropped the following January.

The viewers had a clear choice in Disney, a tried and true family production that not only entertained the kiddies but reminded their parents of youthful exploits and watching Mickey Mouse at the local Bijou on Saturday afternoons. Zimbalist and "The FBI" taught law and order at a time when it seemed that America's youth had abandoned its collective senses and revolution and anarchy might come about any day. It was the beginning of America's rearming the home that would lead to the arsenal that the private citizenry has available today to protect the family castle from enemies seen and unseen. Had "M*A*S*H" aired during the mid-fifties along with *I Love Lucy* and *American Bandstand*, Alan Alda would not have been its star. McCarthyism was the unwritten law of the land. One either subscribed to it out of fear or from dedication. Few openly opposed the senator from Wisconsin while at his peak. Alan Alda, by philosophical belief, at the time (only a teenager) totally subscribed to Joe McCarthy's "Communist in every closet" thesis. He said, "I recalled thinking how right the senator was. We ought to rid our country of subversives."

The die was cast. Would the viewing public opt for old standards or would it embrace the irreverence of a series that many considered antiestablishment, antiwar, and a sacrilege to the thousands of young men who gave their life in Korea? Any number of conservative critics (and some not so conservative) held back any praise, even though they privately confessed to having enjoyed the advance CBS screenings of the show.

Gene Reynolds, a year after it was certain that the show was a hit and could sustain itself in prime-time television, readily admitted an "iffiness" about its success. Alan, on the other hand, saw it differently when the show moved from Sunday nights at eight to Saturday at seven-thirty. The show never did knock its competitors out of the box on Sundays but showed that it could be the number-one fare for the time slot if properly placed.

In an interview with *The New York Times*, Alan said, "I expected we'd be a hit sooner than we were. I never had any doubts about the series."

Reynolds was more conservative: "There was considerable doubt about the move when it was first made. Its popularity surprised everybody, but I see no problem with the coming season, now that the war in Vietnam is over." He also admitted there would have been problems had the war in Vietnam been the subject of the series because of the split in the country over our involvement in the Southeast Asian conflict.

Television critics and political analysts endeavor to cut through rhetoric and get into the meat of a situation. The meat, as many in the media saw it, was the ultraliberal, dovelike "better red than dead" philosophy of the Jane Fondas and other anti-Vietnam War advocates trying to send a message to the country via a thinly disguised situation comedy whose underlying theme might not be pro-American. Alan's response to such criticisms was immediate. He argued that the media was comparing "M*A*S*H" (and Korea) with the Vietnam conflict and then soundly denounced such a conclusion. His series, he contended, was designed to show that war—any war—was an inhumane attack on mankind and should be abolished. Still, critics of "M*A*S*H" continued to nit-pick about the show until the Vietnam War came to an end.

Alan has always been willing to credit others for the success of the show, but crew and cast alike know that Alda had the *last* word on every production. Once asked why the show was so good, he said, "Larry Gelbart, who is a comedy genius, the Mozart of the joke, either writes or rewrites every show. He works night and day. Then producer Gene Reynolds has a great visual sense and there is a feeling of believability. Finally, the cast really likes each other." Still, the cast had its moments of disagreement.

During the first two years of the show, Jackie Cooper directed thirteen episodes of "M* A*S*H." Like Cooper, Gene Reynolds had also been a child actor. They had known each other around Hollywood, and according to Jackie, he gave Reynolds the opportunity to direct the pilot of "Hennessy," which boosted Reynolds' directorial career. Reynolds also credits Jackie with giving him a chance to show his mettle as a director. Gene repaid Jackie's confidence in his ability by hiring him to direct more than a dozen segments of "M*A*S*H." His opinion of Jackie was important in light of events that would transpire during the course of his directing chores on "M*A*S*H" and afterward.

In Jackie's book, *Please Don't Shoot My Dog,* from which he has so graciously permitted me to quote, Gene says: "Jackie's enthusiasm is unique. He's been acting more than fifty years, but when he comes to work, he's read the script, and he's thought about it, and he comes on the set full of enthusiasm. It's almost a manic quality. He gets so fired up, and in these days that's memorable...."

Something else that Gene observed about Jackie is important: "He's always been a strong personality. Strong and aggressive. The problem of people who are aloof comes out of timidity."

Gene's confidence in Cooper was well placed. Jackie won an Emmy (his first) for directing a "M*A*S*H" segment.

Jackie's experience with "M*A*S*H" was rewarding from a director's chair, yet he found Alan Alda, in the long haul, a disappointment. Alda was no stranger to Jackie. When Cooper was preparing to direct the feature film *Stand Up and Be Counted*, he sent Alan a script and considered him for the male lead in the film. Jackie later flew back to the East Coast to confer with Alan on the script as well as to come to terms with the producers on the matter of Alan's salary and other details. Jackie agreed with Alan that there were problems with the script, but he was committed to directing the film, his very first full-length motion picture for the big screen, and wanted to bring it off in the best manner possible. Alan felt the story line was anti-equal rights and made fun of the feminist movement. Jackie saw his point and hoped that changes could be made in the script to accommodate the actor and they could get on with the picture. Mike Frankovich, the producer, refused to permit the changes Alan requested and Alan refused to do the film, as did Sally Kellerman. Jackie never argued with their decision to walk away from the project. The film was eventually completed with Gary Lockwood and Jacqueline Bisset in the roles originally slated for Alda and Kellerman.

When Jackie came into the "M* A*S*H" situation as a director, he expected to find the same Alan Alda he had known before: a man of high principles, amenable to compromise, and "a team man." That, of course, is the image that Alda strives to portray at all times—just one of the guys. On the surface, that's what Jackie initially found. But he soon discovered that "beneath that serene surface, things were different." Jackie had a difficult time believing that Alda did not like him personally. There was no reason for that attitude, so he couldn't understand some of Alan's actions and his lack of interest in the shows. Alan's reputation was of someone who was totally enmeshed in his series, involved in every detail of shooting—in essence having the final say on every bit of dialogue and camera movement. Jackie said, "Alan was determinedly uninvolved. He never ventured an opinion on things that did not directly concern him." When Jackie argued a point with another actor, Alan seemed to deliberately sever himself from the situation, avoiding all discussions that might be pertinent to the "overall" story of a particular week's shooting.

Jackie totally misunderstood Alan's non-commitment to mean that he was leaving the director totally in charge and would follow direction as given. Cooper, having starred in more than one series himself, knew that the star bears the onus of a production because that is who the public will blame if anything goes wrong. Cooper's intent was to work closely with Alan because, by so doing, there would be an aura of cooperation throughout the production company, thus producing the finest show possible.

Cooper's rapport with the crew was quite friendly, he says. He knew the interests of the various crew members and always tried to talk to them about something personal to which they could relate, thereby creating a "family" atmosphere on the set. It is customary in films, and often in television, for the director or star to toss a wrap party on the last day of shooting. With Jackie, that was a carry-over from the big wrap parties that were given by the studio at the end of filming on a motion picture, when all the Hollywood press corps was invited and treated like stars themselves—almost invariably guaranteeing a film a good send-off in the papers. It was a studio write-off and there is no better way to grab publicity.

On the "M*A*S*H" wraps, either Jackie or Gene Reynolds or Larry Gelbart usually tossed a small party for the cast and crew. Jackie remembered that "On 'M*A*S*H' the star's contribution was conspicuously absent."

Stars are the highest salaried members of a television or motion-picture crew. It is customary—with extremely rare exception—for the star to present gifts to their lesser members on a film or series at Christmastime. Jackie remembers the first Christmas he worked on "M*A*S*H."

"Alan wished everybody a Merry Christmas." That was it, according to Cooper.

Whatever was going on between Alda and Cooper created other cast problems. McLean Stevenson came to Jackie and announced that henceforth he was going to do only one take on a shot. Jackie was shocked. He saw Stevenson's demand as "the most unprofessional conduct ... I have ever seen in more than fifty years in the business." Stevenson also requested that he be favored in all master shots in the future so that he wouldn't have to repeat the scene again. When Jackie balked, Stevenson went to Reynolds and Gelbart and complained. He was given instructions to obey the director on the set. According to Cooper, Stevenson's behavior grew even worse.

Jackie, like any good director, would take an actor aside if he had some criticism to avoid embarrassing someone in front of the rest of the cast and crew. He was more than a little surprised when McLean Stevenson began to criticize him openly on the set. Hoping that Alan, the star, could smooth things out, he asked him to speak to Stevenson. Alan refused. Jackie was beginning to sense that perhaps his star was in some way involved in the dissension on the set. "Alan Alda remained aloof, above it all, so cliques and wounds developed."

It appeared that the other actors as well were attempting to express temperament that is reserved for "superstars." Gary Burghoff complained about motivations in the script; Loretta Swit criticized the script, arguing that Hot Lips wouldn't say the words that were written for her to speak or that she wouldn't react this way or that. It was enough to drive any director crazy—if Cooper's remembrances are accurate—and there has been little to refute him except Alda's response of "not wanting to get involved in a dichotomy with Cooper" about what went on during the shooting of the segments Jackie directed.

The stars were divided into two camps, according to Cooper. While McLean Stevenson, Gary Burghoff, and Loretta Swit behaved abominably, Larry Linville and Wayne Rogers were professionals at all times, leaving Alan to stand aside and let the pot boil, as it were. Alda's response to Jackie's appeals for harmony on the set was to head for his own dressing room, where he hibernated until matters simmered down.

Jackie could not fault Alan on the set, however. He found him totally cooperative in any matter that involved *him personally*. He took direction well and often had suggestions and ideas that improved the scene being shot.

The major blowup between Jackie and Alda came over a script involving the use of guns. It was customary for the executives and actors to sit down and go over the script for the next week's episode. In one particular script, the use of guns was called for (actually the firearms competed with the actors for attention). The script involved an enemy sniper taking potshots at the 4077th field hospital. A call is sent out for help and an American helicopter arrives on the scene to bring a soldier, who shoots the offender. Alda, as Hawkeye, does the humanitarian thing (seldom done in actual combat): He goes out in the bush to treat the wounded sniper.

Alda refused to participate in the scene. "I am against violence in any form," he said. Everybody was astonished. They were, after all, shooting a series involving a war. Another irony was the fact that Alda had just the night before starred in a television movie opposite Ruth Gordon in which he played the role of a sheriff—a gun-toting sheriff. This was pointed out by Jackie Cooper. Alan said, yes, that was true, but it was part of the costume required for the role.

Larry Gelbart said, "Yes, but you drew your revolver in that film. You didn't draw any other part of your costume."

Alda insisted that the character he played would never draw a gun. It was merely part of the props. Maybe, Jackie said, but the viewers at home didn't know that. "They just saw you draw it." He refused to act the part as written. A compromise was arrived at, which did not suit the director. Alda agreed to go ahead with the shooting if the onus was placed on the army, not an individual GI. So the helicopter became an airborne armored tank, a gunship armed to the teeth. So far as Cooper was concerned, the whole situation was out of context and totally unrealistic. The gunship would have blasted the sniper into so many bits and pieces that Alda not only would not have been able to treat him but would have had difficulty finding any part of him to treat. Alan had his way, and over Cooper's objections he shot the scene. Alda had convinced Gelbart and Reynolds that he was correct and Cooper was wrong.

From that point on, Jackie Cooper was no longer the total boss, as a director should be. Alda had made it pointedly clear that what he wanted, he got. It was never the same for Jackie again. Alan had totally humiliated him, and everybody knew it. As Jackie recalls, "From then on cooperation became merely a word." Loretta gave him lessons in equality for women, Burghoff tried to teach him acting (although he was a star many years before Burghoff was even thought of), while Alan ignored Cooper except when necessary. Throughout the entire chaotic situation Jackie maintained his rapport with the crew and also with Larry Linville and Wayne Rogers.

With half a dozen additional shows to direct under his contract with Reynolds and Fox, Jackie made every effort to salvage some sort of friendly feeling between Alan and himself. He also sat down with the other actors and tried to give them the benefit of his many years as an actor, reminding them that they had been chosen for their roles because they were *good actors* involved in a funny show. They were not, he assured them, comedians in the same vein as a Carl Reiner. He sincerely wanted harmony on the set.

Although Alan ignored Jackie most of the time during the rest of the week, on the last day, when all of the shooting was finished, he requested that Cooper meet with him off the set, behind a cyclorama next to the M*A*S*H sound stage at Fox studios.

It was at this time the thorn in Alda's ego emerged. Quoting directly from Jackie's book, we pick up with Alan speaking:

"I want to tell you something," he began. "You have no idea what kind of people we are. How dare you say the producers should have gotten a funny man like Carl Reiner in the show?"

Jackie attempted to explain to Alda that he had not been listening to the conversation or he would have known that's not what he said.

Alan ignored him and continued to speak. "Nobody here appreciates your sense of humor."

"Then why does the crew laugh?"

"Because they're kissing your ass. And furthermore, I want you to understand one thing—you're not the star of this show."

The cat was finally out of the bag. Apparently, Alda was jealous of Jackie's popularity. Jackie went to Reynolds and Larry Gelbart and was ready to quit, even though he had further commitments to the show. They discouraged this and Jackie did finish out his directorial assignments, although he and Alan never spoke again except on business. There can be no doubt that both were relieved when their relationship came to an end. It is interesting to note, however, that Jackie Cooper won an Emmy for one of the shows he directed during that period of stress.

The two had words once more before they parted company. Jackie Cooper, a high-ranking commissioned officer in the U.S. Navy, has for years helped the navy's Christmas promotions by asking and getting stars to do promos for the boys in the navy. Most stars do that—send radio and television holiday messages to the boys away from home. Both Wayne Rogers and McLean Stevenson helped out. Alan flatly refused. He claimed that would be encouraging sailors to prolong the Vietnam War.

Jackie asked, "You mean [sending a message to] some eighteen-year-old kid in a gun turret is encouraging the war?"

Alan said, yes, he was, and that he, Alda, would have no part in that.

Cooper could not resist responding. "Well, okay, then," Jackie said, "maybe you'd like to send a little message to the enemy."

Alda, obviously incensed, strode away.

Alan, asked about his conflict with Jackie Cooper, claims that Jackie is trying to trade on his celebrity in order to sell books. That amuses almost anybody who hears it because Jackie Cooper has been making people happy with his great performances since before Alan Alda was born or his father was made into one of Jack Warner's stable of stars.

CHAPTER 11

With the onset of "M*A*S*H" and the popularity of the series and its stars, Alan's attitude changed. To some discerning eyes, the change was quite perceptible. He sought and enjoyed being a star, but the upsurge of fans was not part of that enjoyment. He claims to have had nightmares in which crowds of people were chasing him. He explained in a 1981 *New York Times Magazine* interview with Carey Winfrey that "a large part of my daily life involved people following me in their cars, chasing me down the street, literally coming to get me." Interesting, since a large part of Alda's daily life is spent rehearsing, acting, writing, and directing with very little exposure to the public at large.

In any event, had the handwriting on the wall been accurate, Alan would not have had to worry about nightmares or fans because the initial season of "M*A*S*H" followed on the heels of a long-forgotten attempt to bring *The King and I* to television in the form of a series. The lead-in to that first season of "M*A*S*H" was a trickle. How does one pick up an audience that has already fled to another channel? The truth was that "M*A*S*H" and all those good old guys of the 4077th Mobile Army Surgical Hospital were almost abandoned behind the lines when the January cut came at the networks in early 1973, after the death rattle of the Nielsen ratings had been heard. Most knowledgeable media and television critics, as well as executives, credit Alan

Alda with the continuation of "M*A*S*H" past the first thirteen weeks of keeping afloat in deep water.

The survival of "M* A*S*H" midway through the first season was Alan's first true Hollywood triumph, and knowing how fickle the movie and television industries can be, he moved rapidly to assure continuance and assert his authority as the star of the show. From January 1973 until the end of the series, there has never been a moment's doubt in anyone's mind who actually controlled every aspect of "M*A*S*H." That authority has belonged always to Alan. He has wielded it with the strength, if not always the wisdom, of a reigning monarch sitting on a throne beset by scurrilous pretenders bent on treachery.

Even during the clashes with Jackie Cooper, the producers tried to find a compromise rather than anger their star. After all, Jackie was merely one of dozens of competent directors capable of following Alan's ideas during the production of "M*A*S*H" segments. The problem was that Jackie's track record was better than Alan's over a longer span of years. Jackie makes it clear that when Alan *did not* get his way, he went out of his way to be uncooperative and disruptive.

The point to make here, obviously, is that when it came time to decide at what hour and day "M*A*S*H" would air during the second season, Alan Alda was in the forefront with his ideas and insistence (in lieu of demands). He knew the network scheduling by heart. There was only one place for his program to air and that was on Saturday nights, sandwiched in between two of the all-time television hits. On the front end of the prime-time slot was Norman Lear's "dare to be different," "All in the Family" and the pseudo-sophisticated forerunner of the innocuous and inane "Laverne & Shirley" of today, "The Mary Tyler Moore Show," was on the other.

From the outset, one mustn't forget that "M*A*S*H" was and is an excellent show. There is a comparable series on the air now, comparable in the sense that somebody had to believe in it past the first half season. That show is "Hill Street Blues." Early Nielsen ratings were so low the show might as well have been sitting on the bottom of the lake. Because someone believed in it, "Hill Street Blues" is now one of television's top-rated shows and has won numerous Emmys. Such was the inauspicious beginning of "M*A*S*H." Just as NBC's Fred Silverman believed in "Hill Street Blues," Alan Alda believed in "M*A*S*H" even more than the producers of the show, who had serious doubts that the timing was proper for a war spoof.

"M*A*S*H" managed to do what no other war series had ever been able to accomplish. While it poked fun at the bureaucracy of the military, it managed to expose the raw nerve endings of human beings under pressure in blood-soaked operating rooms, under the most primitive conditions, without nauseating the American psyche. It established Alan Alda as a major television star, not so much because he was a great actor but probably more because he took gory situations and made the participants come off as real human beings with believable problems.

The first season of "M*A*S*H" reveals the following data: All shows were produced by Gene Reynolds. Writers were:

> *Larry Gelbert (7); Laurence Marks (5); Burt Styler (2); Hal Dresner (2); Bob Klane (2); Bruce Shelly and David Ketchum (1); Jerry Mayer (1); Sheldon Keller (1); Carl Kleinschmitt (1); Alan Alda; Sid Dorfman (1). Directors were: Gene Reynolds; William Wiard (4); Michael O'Herlihy (1); Terry Becker (1); Hy Averback (3); E. W. Swackhamer (1); Don Weis (3); Lee Phillips (1); Bruce Bilson (1); James Sheldon (1); Earl Bellamy (2); Jackie Cooper (3).*

Obviously, during the first season a great deal of experimenting was done with directors, looking for that right combination. Reynolds directed the first episode but did not direct again until the thirteenth. Jackie Cooper came into the picture with the sixteenth. There were sixty-six male guest stars and thirty-eight female ones during the first season, but no women were included in either the writing or directing credits.

Even at the end of two years the show was not in the top twenty, though it had climbed considerably upward from the cellar position of the first year, and the indicators all pointed toward a steady climb in the years to come. "M*A*S*H" was beginning to capture the fancy of the American television viewer.

By the end of the second season, certain aspects of the series had jelled and would remain the same throughout the run. Also, the male domination of the show continued. The regulars remained the same. All second season shows were co-produced by Gene Reynolds and Larry Gelbart.

Writers were:

> *Larry Gelbert (14); Laurence Marks (13); Jerry Mayer (1); Alan Alda (1); Robert Klane (1) (co-writer with Alda); Carl Kleinschmitt (1); Marc Mandel (1); McLean Stevenson (1); Richard M. Powell (1); Bernard Dilbert (1); Linda Bloodworth (1); Mary Kay Place (1) (co-writer with Bloodworth); Ed Jurist (1); Sheldon Keller (2); Erik Tarloff (1); John Reiger (1); Gary Markowitz (1) (co-writer with Reiger). Many of these scripts were co-written with Gelbart. Directors: Jackie Cooper (9); Norman Tokar (1); William Wiard (2); Don Weis (5); Gene Reynolds (2); Hy Averback (2); Alan Alda (1).*

Although Alan wrote two segments, one each in the first two seasons, the second season marked his first directorial chore on "M*A*S*H." He was making a move toward that dominance over the show he soon had. In season two, there were fifty-eight male and thirty-eight female guest stars. Behind the camera, women writers appeared for the first time. A segment entitled "Hot Lips and Empty Arms" was written by Linda Bloodworth and Mary Kay Place (who later became such a hit in the "Mary Hartman, Mary Hartman" series). It wasn't much of a showing for women, but most women in the television industry saw it as a beginning.

"M*A*S*H" ignored all the rules of network protocol and etiquette of the past. Its characters were more strangers in a commune than a closely knit family, the norm for television series fare. Alan Alda described his character as "a sexual Archie Bunker" who, in spite of showing a great comradeship to his fellow actors, was a decided cynic who hated the war (as did most of the other characters). There were absolutely no tried and true indicators to foresee the tremendous success the show would eventually become. Most knowledgeable heads in the television industry gave educated guesses that when the Vietnam War finally ended "M*A*S*H" would fade as quickly as last summer's tan. That did not happen, catching many prophets at a flat-footed loss to explain their doubts.

Although it was vehemently denied by the producers, the general consensus was that "M*A*S*H" was intended to give succor to those who were opposed to the Vietnam War. Alan Alda was most certainly an opponent of that particular conflict. Alda stated that "the police action in Korea was simply a rehearsal for the Vietnam War." The nuances of his style both as a writer and actor reflected his antiwar feelings from the onset. A man who was always quite determined, Alan found a method by which he could make his voice reach millions of listeners.

"M* A*S*H" was the antithesis of "All in the Family" and gave viewers an opportunity, for the first time in television history at least, to make direct contrasts in their watching habits as well as having an opportunity (some say) to see the error of Archie Bunker's ways and the right of Alda's in "M*A*S*H."

While Alan was exerting his own energies toward making "M*A*S*H" a success, his father, having left the United States for Rome, was busy on the Continent. He and Flora had moved back to Italy in 1970 when doctors indicated that she had a slight case of emphysema and advised that the smog-ridden environs of New York and Los Angeles would seriously affect her health. Although Bob's work was in the United States, he did not hesitate to preserve the health of his wife.

He did not abandon America, however, and commuted back and forth across the Atlantic when there was work for him to do in television or films. As a security measure, he and Flora opened a very intimate dinner club in Rome, the Il Den. Featuring great food and a piano bar, the club seated fifty at most, and it didn't take long for word to spread that Il Den was *the* place to dine when in Rome. Whoever happened to be in town at any given time, including the host himself, would get up and entertain. Show people loved it, as did the Romans.

Bob Alda also made films in Italy. During the early seventies he made *Death in Rome* for Carlo Ponti, the husband of screen beauty Sophia Loren, costarring with Marcello Mastroianni and Richard Burton. While making this picture his old friend from the days of *Rhapsody in Blue*, Oscar Levant, died, which cast a pall over Alda's life. He also worked in Paris doing *Snake in the Grass*, costarring Henry Fonda and Yul Brynner. It was a "film" production, since Bob Alda was at the time the official television spokesman for Kodak and Fonda was representing GAF. The two made much fun out of that bit of trivia. *Snake in the Grass* became *Le Serpent*, released as an Avco-Embassy film in the United States in 1974.

"M*A*S*H" boasted a real doctor on the set at all times in order to guarantee authentic medical lingo in the operating room, where much of the action and dialogue took place. During an interview with Dick Lochte for *TV Guide* in February 1973, at the end of the very first season, Lochte ascertained that Alda probably would have welcomed the good M.D. had they been shooting in a real combat situation. Lochte pointed out that it was not so much that Alda is a hypochondriac off-camera, but his whole history as an actor has been tinged with impending disaster. To that point in his career, he had become the victim of numerous bruises and injuries, which include being burned, beaten, and falling down any number of flights of stairs. He has been asked to dive into shark-infested waters (which he did), wade through quicksand, and allow himself to be used as a human football by the Detroit Lions while making *Paper Lion*. Two convicts once held a razor to his throat (although it was later revealed to be a gag—Alda didn't think it was such a great joke at the time). While making the pilot for "M*A*S*H," he had to be constantly cautioned to bend his six-foot-two frame to keep from being decapitated by the whirling copter blades.

He revealed to Lochte that away from work he led a totally non-perilous existence in Leonia, New Jersey, where his profile was that of the near perfect insurance risk. Alda doesn't smoke nor drink to excess—the perfect American male in the eyes of the underwriter. During that first season, McLean Stevenson revealed, "Alan has a tremendous amount of concentration, more intense than I've ever seen before. He doesn't just act out a role, he throws himself into it completely."

While making the film *The Extraordinary Seaman* for John Frankenheimer, he recalls that "One of Frankenheimer's hobbies is risking actors' lives. First he made me walk across quicksand. Then I had to jump into the ocean with a bunch of sharks. He kept telling me there weren't any, but we'd all seen them. I hired some Mexican divers to go in ahead of me with their knives ready.... My last thought as I jumped from the ship was 'I'm leaping on top of people with knives in their hands.'" During Alan's interview with Dick Lochte, he practically insisted that the world know that he lived in Leonia, New Jersey, which he reckoned to be about fifteen minutes from Broadway (thirty minutes shorter than George M. Cohan's tuneful distance.) "New York," Alan complained, "is such an anonymous city. In Los Angeles," he also complained, "you have to make appointments to see people. In Leonia, you just walk over to a neighbor's house. You get involved in community projects, help frame the politics of the town. It's all very satisfying." This great dissertation by Alan on the merits of Leonia, New Jersey, brought no small amount of frustration to Mr. Lochte. When I wrote to Dick requesting permission to use the material in his story, he responded with the following additional information:

A little bit of background—it was one of my very first assignments for the *Guide* and also one of Alda's first interviews for a magazine of that size circulation. He did not hesitate to mention his hometown ... so I used it. "M*A*S*H" then debuted, Alda became a major star, and I was chagrined to hear him say, one night on "The Merv Griffin Show," that one price he paid for the fame was that he had to put up with people camping on his front lawn. They'd learned of his address from an article in a national magazine.

Between the first and second season, *To Kill a Clown* was released. It was a film Alan had completed in 1972 and it was another instance where he was close to danger—or so he thought. "I had a scene with wild dogs," he says, "and I was warned that they would be vicious, so I expected the worst." They turned out to be tame animals. The film was more dog than the four-legged actors.

Not all of the actors on "M*A*S*H" came from the luxuriant "my father was a movie star" background, nor were they all privy to as much travel and high-echelon elbow-rubbing as Alan. As late as 1971 Gary Burghoff, a then-unemployed actor, was courting his future wife—coming to call in a battered old milk truck. Janet Gayle, formerly of Santa Monica, California, recalled their honeymoon in the cold backcountry of British Columbia in Canada. "We were without luxuries," she says, "there were no hotels, and the two of us slept in twenty-degree weather in bedrolls in the back of Gary's milk wagon. It was the next thing to dying."

Gary was drawing seventy-five-dollars-a-week unemployment checks from the state of California and living in a small beach apartment in Malibu (not in the famous Malibu Colony). Woefully disconsolate, he never let his agent forget for a moment that he was now among the unemployed and he, the agent, better get the lead out and find him some work. Unemployment checks only last so long. The Burghoff luck changed. He had been in the original Robert Altman production of *M*A*S*H*, but still had to test for the part of Radar O'Reilly before he was hired to do the same role in the series. During his "at liberty" period, Burghoff began to study birds and became so expert that he has been applauded by ornithologists, the Los Angeles Zoo, veterinarians, lifeguards, and many southern California beachcombers. His expertise came in the form of knowing the various species that inhabit the coastal areas of Southern California and, more importantly, starting a rescue service, recovering and treating birds in distress along the beach areas—oil-soaked, snagged on fishhooks, broken-winged, aged, diseased, or otherwise in trouble and unable to help themselves. He picked up the apt title of "Birdman of Malibu." It was not unusual for his wife to suddenly discover that she had to share their humble abode with various basket cases, running the gamut from green heron (victim of pesticide poisoning) to stray dogs, cats, and brush rabbits.

Gary Burghoff spoke quite honestly to *TV Guide's* Al Stump: "Some people think I'm kind of strange. I don't mix much socially. I don't think I'm regarded as a wierdo, but people wonder what I'm all about. What they don't know is that even if they knew me—they wouldn't really know me."

Gary has ESP. He often hears the telephone ring before it rings and has picked up the receiver before anyone else can hear the ring. It is interesting to note that Radar also has an uncanny ability to sense events before they happen, although Burghoff swears that this is mere coincidence. Like Alda, Burghoff shies away from the big city. "New York," he says, "is an insane town. I live on the beach now, as far from downtown Hollywood and L.A. as possible."

Burghoff was as dedicated to his character in "M*A*S*H" as Alda or anyone else in the cast. He sees Radar as someone struggling to survive not only war and war psychosis but the danger of becoming an object of ridicule (as Jamie Farr has done with great delight in the series). He sees Radar as being young and moving in very fast company, but sharper in many ways than some of his superiors. Burghoff doesn't particularly like to take direction. He knows his role and plays it the way he sees it. That so irritated Wayne Rogers, who plays the boozing Trapper John (or did in the beginning), that he threw a chair at Burghoff during a scene. Gary also had his screaming sessions with McLean Stevenson who loomed "feet" over him.

Burghoff dismisses such things as all part of the day's work. "I claimed that our new director hadn't bothered to study the previous thirteen shows. He was letting people walk on my lines. Mac Stevenson took me aside and gave me a blast, so I told him off."

Stevenson told him right back. "I don't have to take that kind of shit from you, kid!" Burghoff left the set and returned to his dressing room to cool off. He admits that the soft approach, which Alda used several times to resolve conflicts in which Gary became a participant, worked better than yelling. "I don't like to be yelled at by anyone," he says.

Burghoff was once asked point-blank if any of the actors on "M*A*S*H" had a star complex. His response was quite pragmatic. "We all feel we are stars, if getting mail has anything to do with it. We each get over two hundred letters a week. And we get paid enough to feel good."

The publicity department at Twentieth Century-Fox says that Jamie Farr was hired for one day's work as a phony transvestite bucking for a Section Eight (mentally unbalanced discharge) during an early episode in the first season of "M*A*S*H." The role he created was that of Corporal Klinger, who would go to all lengths—skirts, of course—in an effort to escape the madness of a front-line hospital in Korea. He so surprised the studio brass by the public response to his appearance that he was brought back to appear in six subsequent segments during the first season. That led to a dozen appearances on the second season, and finally, by the time the third season came around, his role had been tried and found non-offensive and he became a regular and has been ever since.

There is no secret about Farr's role. Milton Berle has been making a living in drag for years, as have any number of successful actors. No one will forget Jack Benny in *Charley's Aunt*, a drag role that has been mimicked by every comedian (and some non-comedians) in the business.

Loretta Swit, the only woman in a sustaining role in "M*A*S*H" is far removed from Hot Lips Houlihan. A blonde, green-eyed Polish-American from Passaic, New Jersey, she shuts her eyes tightly at the very sight of blood. Loretta feels that her character and herself person-ally represent two stages in the liberation of the American female—twenty years apart. "At the time of the Korean War, just to have an affair with a married man was a mark of liberation in itself." Hot Lips never admits that she lusts after Frank, which is in and of itself part of the comedy surrounding her role. Houlihan has chosen to establish herself as a person, Swit says, in that she hasn't accepted the traditional housewife-and-children role without question. The army life was by choice without the consent or permission of any man, and she is a tip-top technician in her job.

In her private life, she fights to prove that she is not "a Barbie doll," but a person, a woman, an actress who is associated with a series of which she is extremely proud. She once went on a national tour to help promote "M*A*S*H" (back when "M*A*S*H" needed promotion) and a radio interviewer made the mistake of asking her the inane question, "Do you drink your milk hot or cold?" Loretta bristled with her im-mediate response: "I don't drink milk at all, but why don't you ask me about the children's book I wrote?" For all practical purposes, she had reduced the interviewer to ashes.

If Alan has been the point of raised eyebrows in the case of equality for women on the show, Loretta never has. In 1974, Swit's costumer, a woman, suddenly announced that she was leaving the show because "I don't receive the same salary as men costumers who are doing the same thing. It isn't fair." Loretta agreed and put the ball in motion by complaining to the producers, which eventually led to Twentieth Century-Fox paying both sexes the same salary for the same job in costuming.

Alan immediately took Loretta under his wing when she was signed to do "M*A*S*H." Loretta laughs when she recalls those early days on location when the temperature would drop fifteen degrees in a few minutes and they would all huddle together to keep warm early in the morning. "Alan, who is heavily involved in what he calls 'the human rights movement,' treated me like a kid sister. One of the points he made clear to me was that it was not incongruous for me to play an exploited sex object like Hot Lips in 'M*A*S*H,' since it was a period piece. 'After all,' he said, 'you could play a murderess without believing in killing.'"

Loretta, perhaps because of the Alda influence, has become very active in the effort to clean up the Polish-American image, which she believes has been subject to ridicule and bad jokes for too long. She makes speeches for the League of Polish Americans and, like singer Bobby Vinton, believes Polish Power should come from Polish pride. On "M*A*S*H" she is the in-house troubleshooter, always able to sooth a ruffled ego or find the solution to differences between the giant bantam roosters who make up the male coterie on the show.

It was no small feat for Gene Reynolds and Larry Gelbart together with executive producer Burt Metcalfe to keep so much high-strung talent in the same corral for so long. It is a minor miracle that they got through two seasons without a major break—that came before the second season was completed. That would be the beginning of the end of that "old gang of 'M*A*S*H,'" and by the time the eventual smoke cleared, three original stalwarts of the show exited in one stage of "huff" or another. More and more Alan continued to emerge as "Mr. Big" in every facet of the "M*A*S*H" production. It is little wonder that it came to be commonly referred to as "The Alan Alda Show."

CHAPTER 12

McLean Stevenson was visibly disgruntled by the middle of the second season and made no bones about it. Why he finally exited the show is a matter of just whose story you are prone to believe. Although there was a production company, Twentieth Century-Fox was the overlord of the show and above it was the CBS Television network. The then-CBS programming chief, Fred Silverman, who attained fame at ABC and some sort of infamy later at NBC, was the single man who was in a position to push buttons that meant life or death to a series. Fred Silverman alone made the decision to keep "M*A*S*H" on the air, thus assuring Stevenson a job past the first and second seasons.

The Fox executives proffered the story that Stevenson wanted a higher salary, a story immediately refuted by McLean, who stated quite emphatically that he had been offered double his salary if he would stay on the show for the run of his contract, which was originally for five years. A compromise was negotiated whereby Stevenson would stay on the show an additional year at his original salary if Fox would allow him to cancel out his final two years without a court contest. So, at the beginning of the third season, McLean's position on "M*A*S*H" was that of lame-duck character. Stevenson has always insisted that his gripe was not with the "M*A*S*H" production company, but with Twentieth Century-Fox itself. He contended that the big studio didn't give one damn how the actors felt, that all he was asking for was decent dressing quarters not only for himself but for the entire cast. In summertime, during the hottest months of the year, while the fall segments were being filmed, the stage temperatures were often well over the hundred-degree mark, and he wanted some cool air vented onto the sound stage. On location, he contended, conditions were even worse.

"I wasn't looking for a parking lot for my car," he said, "merely a place to go to the bathroom." Stevenson was not the only member of the cast complaining, but he was certainly the most vocal. He simply did not understand how a show getting ready to begin a third season could be so badly handled when it came to ordinary and necessary facilities for human beings to function. Stevenson did not even hang around for the wrap party, which is almost always thrown by the studio or production company as a way of saying good-bye at the end of the season. He had already been humiliated beyond belief by the manner in which he exited the show when the final segment for the year was shot.

It had been assumed that, as Henry Blake, he would be transferred out of the unit and reassigned to another base. The *real* ending had been secretly written, placed in a sealed envelope, and opened only on the day his "disposition" scene was shot. Rather than being transferred, he was discharged and killed off in a plane crash on his way back to the States. The entire cast was in shock. The exception was Alda, who avoided the incident, just as he had with the unpleasantries when Jackie Cooper had been directing.

In any event, the script was written in a manner that precluded Stevenson ever coming back to the show again. His character was dead, and that was that. Stevenson said it was the finality of his end on the show that hurt the most. That's understandable.

Wayne Rogers, another of the originals on the show, also left at the end of the third season. His exit, however, was more bombastic than Stevenson's. Rogers left in a headline-making flurry of accusations from both himself and Twentieth Century-Fox, ending in multimillion-dollar lawsuits filed by both parties. Having been signed before Alda to do the show, Rogers' role should have been on an equal footing with that of Alda, but more and more Hawkeye Pierce was emerging as *the* big character in the series. Rogers really preferred having a series of his own where he would be the star, making his own decisions and where, if he didn't like something, he could change it. He has a temper and is quick to show it, just as he can instantly forget an incident and suddenly smile as if nothing ever happened. When he threw a chair at Gary Burghoff during a script argument, he was the first to break out in laughter when, at later script conferences, Alan Alda would request a member of the crew to "Bring Mr. Rogers' chair, please."

Rogers did not leave "M*A*S*H" over a salary dispute, as was supposedly the case with Stevenson. Always an astute businessman, Wayne was much more interested in the financial world than in acting. Even today, in addition to his 2500-acre vineyard, he has his own business management firm, which boasts such clients as James Caan and Peter Falk.

But he is a man of principles. When Twentieth Century-Fox sued him for $2.9 million for what the studio considered breach of contract, he countersued, accusing the studio of defamation of character and "wrongful interference with economic opportunity." After the headlines and tempers subsided, both sides dropped their suits. Rogers said, "I love 'M*A*S*H' and I love all the great guys I've been working with, but it's time I move on. I sure hope people aren't going to think I'm ungrateful, but I've got to do more with my life than just be Trapper John."

If Alan felt any remorse at losing two of his costars at the same time, he never expressed it publicly.

In spite of low ratings during the first season, there were several nominations for Emmys from "M*A*S*H," ten in all, including Alan Alda as best actor in a comedy series, Gary Burghoff and McLean Stevenson for outstanding performances in supporting roles; three nominations for Gene Reynolds in various categories and for Larry Gelbart for writing. Although none of them won anything the night of the awards, it was good exposure for the series. Both the show and Alan Alda were nominated by the Hollywood Foreign Press Association for Golden Globe Awards. The Directors Guild presented Gene Reynolds with an award for the pilot segment, while the Writers Guild honored Larry Gelbart for a segment called "Chief Surgeon Who?"

Alan was very busy picking up an Emmy as best actor in a series following the second complete season of "M* A*S*H." His friend Mary Tyler Moore won as best actress. "M*A*S*H" won best comedy series of the year. All in all it was a great lift toward the beginning of a third season. Alan was suddenly in great demand by the media for interviews. During one such occasion, a fan approached the table where Alan and the writer were lunching and began a dialogue about the film M*A*S*H. When he realized that Alan had a pained reaction to his dissertation he asked, "But you're doing the whole 'M*A*S*H' TV series, aren't you?"

"Yeah," Alda mumbled, "but I didn't have anything to do with the movie." The fellow insisted that Alan closely resembled Hawkeye Pierce from the movie. Alan said, "No, I don't think that's true," becoming more uncomfortable with each additional comment.

"Well," the guy said, "don't you play the surgeon?" He continued on, "My brother-in-law's a surgeon. Up the street here. I gotta go see him in a few minutes. Ha Ha." It is the kind of encounter that stars must contend with, but almost to a man they would rather avoid. After the man departed, Alan said, "I'm surprised. That usually doesn't happen. I have the feeling he simply may not have seen the series much." Alan should have been elated for other reasons, however. He had just learned that "M*A*S*H" was number five in the ratings that week with a 42 percent share of the audience.

More indicative of Alan's increasing power over the show was a comment made by Robert Cross of the Chicago Tribune. "The show," he said, "is secure enough that network big shots can relax and allow

'M*A*S*H' to head in the direction *Alda* (emphasis mine) would like to see it go." This must have pleased Alan since he was definitely not satisfied that "M*A*S*H" was where he wanted it go to at the time. "We are not allowed the same kind of openness that 'All in the Family' is allowed, or 'Maude.' 'All in the Family' is allowed jokes on vasectomy. 'Maude' is allowed whole shows on abortion. We're not interested in saying naughty words, but we ought to at least recognize what is common usage in the culture and stop pretending that we have the innocence of five-year-olds." He stressed that "M*A*S*H" was not an antiwar statement—it was a *pro-life* statement. "We must express sanity," he emphasized, "because war is obviously an insane institution. We at 'M*A*S*H' agree with a long line of American presidents and generals and, umm, other butchers." Alan was beginning to express his opinions with a sharp tongue.

In 1974 Alan, now with a firm footing as a recognized celebrity, came out more openly in favor of the Equal Rights Amendment. There was a possibility that the Illinois legislature would take up the proposed amendment that year, and Alan created quite a furor and picked up a tremendous amount of publicity in the process. In his public statement, made in Chicago, he brought squeals of delight from the women behind the ERA.

"I came here because I'm a feminist," he said, "and I want to help get the Equal Rights Amendment passed in this state." He denied that he was "shopping around for good causes. I don't like to see women being subservient to men." While it is true that he shares the household chores, he declares, "I do the dishes, things like that. My wife chose to give up her career for a while. I choose to bake bread once in a while. My wife chose to devote more time to her children than to a clarinet."

It was the beginning of an almost second career for Alda, pushing the ERA, a cause that would bring him almost as much notoriety as acting.

Alan probably had no idea what a springboard "M*A*S*H" would be for him. By the end of the second season on the air, he was one of the hottest properties in show business, solicited for interviews, guest stints on other shows, and endorsements of causes and products. In addition to all this new attention, he found that CBS was now interested in reading some of his many scripts, which had been accumulating while he solidified his position as an actor. At the end of each season's shooting, Alan returned to Leonia to reestablish himself as a husband and father and to beseech CBS to look at his scripts.

The network showed an interest in a story he had penned concerning New York politics, but it meant that Alan would have to relocate the setting because executives at CBS considered New York to be a city that wouldn't sell to the Nielsen viewers. Alan refused to change the locale because, "I figured it would be better to do it right and not get it on the air than to do it weird and get it on." He now enjoyed the prestige of not having to do creative projects just for money. If he couldn't have it done his way, then his attitude was simply to forget it until another day when perhaps a more responsive network bigwig would see how right he was.

CBS did not close the door on his suggestions, however. The network liked his style of writing and there was some conversation about the possibility of a family- oriented show—a show that would deal with family situations in a humane manner, yet with total candor. He took the idea back to Hollywood as homework when he left the "M*A*S*H" set after a strenuous day and went home to his little apartment on the west side of town. He was being recognized by the people who count as being a man of prolificity in more than one field.

His father was keeping busy in the movie world, filming *Bittersweet Love,* an Avco-Embassy movie that costarred Lana Turner, Robert Lansing, and Celeste Holm—not necessarily the biggest stars of the day, but seasoned actors who could make even a so-so script shine.

With all three children now in school and Alan spending most of his time in Los Angeles, Arlene discovered that she had more extra time on her hands than she knew what to do with, so she began to revive her feelings of creativity, which had been stifled for so much of the past fifteen years or so of marriage. Checking at a Leonia school for adult education, she found she had two options. Either she could take up embroidery or photography. Embroidery sounded too much like confinement to the rocking chair in the parlor, so she opted for the photographic class. She discovered she had the ability to "visualize" what the finished picture would look like, and within a matter of only a few weeks she was producing photographs that were definitely of professional quality.

As the old adage goes, one thing leads to another and before long she was practicing on her clarinet. For the first time in years she was able to be, for part of the day, Arlene Weiss instead of Mrs. Alan Alda, hausfrau to "that actor." She soon organized a local chamber music group, which delighted Alan because there was no leisure-time activity he loved more than having chamber music concerts at his home in the evenings. Arlene went one step further, again with Alan's acquiescence, by joining a symphony orchestra in Connecticut that performed half a dozen concerts a year. It gave her the opportunity to become active as an artist once more without having to give up any of her family duties. She was happier than she had been in years.

Now that Alan was a household name, he was also a man whose face was as recognizable as any national monument. Even though he had appeared on Broadway, in films, and on television for several years, he had been able to maintain a certain amount of anonymity. There had been no "face value" identification among the general public. With the snowballing success of "M*A*S*H," all that changed. And it frightened him. "I remember how strangers reacted to my father after the George Gershwin picture with all that publicity. I didn't want to fall victim to the same process." Now, a minimum of thirty million or so people saw his face each and every week in prime-time television. He admits it was a lot of fun in the beginning, but fans can be and often are obnoxious—actually doing physical damage to celebrities who happen to be the object of their affections at a given moment. Every entertainer who attains superstar status lives in fear of a crazed fan's over-zealous attentions.

Consequently, rather than face the realities of the public streets and restaurants, Alan retreated to his apartment to work on the series he hoped CBS would buy and air. And they did, hiring Alan to produce thirteen episodes of "We'll Get By," half a season's quota for a series.

He was so delighted with the prospect that he gave up his small apartment and purchased a house in Bel-Air, an exclusive community populated by movie-industry people along with oil moguls, eastern potentates, and other assorted procurers of wealth.

The format of "We'll Get By" was out of the Alan Alda family scrapbook, or so many said. It was a comedy set in suburban New Jersey, where Alan maintained his voting residence, and it involved the life and times of the Platt family. George, played by Paul Sorvino, was a practicing attorney. His wife, Liz, played by Mitzi Hoag, stayed home with her three young children like a good suburban housewife. The three Platt children, rounding out the scenario, were played by Devon Scott, Willie Aames, who found stardom on the "Family" series, and Jerry Houser from the hit film *The Summer of '42*. The thirty-minute sit-com premiered on CBS March 6, 1975, and the last segment appeared May 30 of the same year. It was not a long run as series go, but that did not daunt Alan. If anyone was mistaken, it was the network programmers, whose taste was often suspect. For those who thought the program was too autobiographical, Alan merely stated that the problems and cares involved in the short-lived series were the same he had after seventeen years of marriage, but then so did everybody else.

Not having the series extended must have been more than mildly frustrating for Alda. A man who works at appearing calm and collected, he has been known to seethe during an argument involving his beliefs. Wayne Rogers, who had his share of disagreements with Alan during his three years on "M*A*S*H," remembered Alan's tenacity in that regard. "In essence we agreed on the principles of a scene when we worked together, but we usually took different routes to arrive at the same conclusions." Whereas Rogers has a tendency to make decisions on impulse, knowing where he is going instinctively, Alan takes a more deliberate, plodding approach. Says Rogers, "I have a thin skin and expose my emotions more readily. That takes some reining in on my part, controlling my feelings." Alda, on the other hand, is pretty much an engineer with his emotions, planning and thinking problems out to what he considers a logical conclusion. Before leaving "M*A*S*H," Rogers saw Alan in a special light. "He's not a phony. He's real to the core."

Whether he had a hit series away from "M*A*S*H" did not deter Alan from looking ahead, as always, to new and brighter moments. He guest-starred with half a dozen other comedians on a show hosted by Anne Bancroft with a tongue-in-cheek title, "Annie and the Hoods." He was in big comedy company along with the irrepressible Jack Benny, Mel Brooks, Carl Reiner, Gene Wilder, and others. Alan now added viewers to any show he appeared on. He was that nice young man on "M*A*S*H" who drank too much, chased too many women, and epitomized the fantasies of many American males. The women all forgave his character. After all, he was thousands of miles away from home. Why not allow him some diversions from the horrors of war? He simply could not do anything wrong from the public's point of view—and to a large extent that attitude still prevails among his millions of fans.

Another longtime friendship was in the making for Alan. On March 17, 1974, he co-directed with Clark Jones a ninety-minute special for CBS called 6 Rms Riv Vu. Carol Burnett was his costar in this dramatic offering, while her husband, Joe Hamilton, was the producer. The Hamiltons and the Aldas found they had much in common: their mutual interest in causes and issues as well as the industry they found themselves locked into both by choice and demand. Alan was, at the time, very much involved with "We'll Get By" and would bend the ears off anyone who would listen to his feelings about the project. The show had originally been scheduled to premiere on the fall season but was set back until spring. He said, "The show is family life the way it really is. The humor of recognition, not just jokes or bizarre situations. Life itself is funny enough. It will be different from 'The Waltons' or 'Apple's Way.' I wrote six of the first scripts, supervised four others, and probably will direct the final three so that I can see that the characters talk as I intended. It's reality with a sense of humor." He relied on his own children for a great deal of his material. In one discussion with his daughter Beatrice, she stopped in midsentence and said, "Well, I certainly hope you're getting all of this down!"

On April 14, 1975, President Gerald Ford, with his wife, Betty, at his side, made an announcement during a very ceremonious affair that the federal government was one of the worst offenders when it came to fair and equal treatment for women. Among those cheering his statements was the lovably unpredictable surgeon from "M*A*S*H," Alan Alda. The president gave his wife credit for bringing all those inadequacies to his attention. The reception was important because the National Commission on the International Women's Year was having its first meeting the next day. The president added to Alda's pleasure by appointing him and Katharine Hepburn (who was ill and couldn't attend) as new members of the commission. It was a great event for Alan, receiving such an honor from a Republican president when it was generally assumed (based on his liberal philosophies) that Alda was a staunch Democrat. His daughter Elizabeth, then thirteen, was the proudest person in the room when the president made his announcement of the appointments.

Alan brought along not only his daughter, but a few pointed comments about women's rights. "The women's movement," he forthrightly told the assemblage, "affects men as well as women. A man cannot take pleasure in seeing a woman squashed down like a gnat."

It was to be a year of frantic activity on Alan's part in the movement to improve women's status in the country. In addition, "M*A*S*H" was beginning its third season and he appeared on television in several interesting and varied shows. An "ABC Movie of the Week" featured *Playmates*, a comedy about two divorced men who make secret plays for each other's wife. His costars were Doug McClure, as the other husband, along with Connie Stevens and Barbara Feldon, as the two wives. It was frothy and cute and fared well in the ratings. The Mario Thomas special for ABC, which had originally appeared on March 11, 1974, was repeated in January the following year, giving Alan additional exposure to his ever growing coterie. He also hosted a documentary-like special, *Tune in America*, along with a host of liberal-minded Hollywood personalities, including Ed Asner, Lorne Green, Helen Reddy, Della Reese, and Susan Saint James. Although it was labeled a documentary, it was in fact an all-out twenty-and-one-half-hour telethon to raise money for the Democratic party in which celebrities as well as numerous Democratic senators, representatives, governors, and mayors paraded before the cameras.

While Alan was being very political, his father appeared in *The Last Hours Before Morning*, a Charles Fries Production for "NBC Night at the Movies." The Alda family was onstage, except for Antony, who was rarely heard of even though he was as they say, "in the business."

Amid his politicking for the Democratic party, Alan was also speaking out loud and clear for "M*A*S*H," not content that they were home safe as yet. He spread the good word and praised everybody and anybody who might have had anything to do with the renewal of his series. "'All in the Family' and 'The Mary Tyler Moore Show' made 'M*A*S*H' possible," he said. "'All in the Family' dealt with subjects not traditionally fit for comedy, such as death, rape, bigotry. 'Mary Tyler Moore' doesn't deal with subjects, but with human behavior. That's comedy coming out of character. These two shows made 'M*A*S*H possible.' We've gone on from there." *People* magazine agreed. In an article by Barbara Wilkins, she said, "It certainly has—as viewers will realize by the way in which 'M*A*S*H's' McLean Stevenson is being disposed of. Never in the history of U.S. prime-time TV has a major character been written out of the script so brutally." All a part of the futility-of-war message, Wilkins states, which Alda considers the subject of "M*A*S*H."

Alan was furious about the human condition in America when he received his honorary doctorate of humane letters at Saint Peter's College in his adopted state of New Jersey. He approached the podium with withering fire in his eyes and on his lips. "We've had Watergate," he preached, "Vietnam, and cars that fall apart. Movies that poke their fingers into gore for the fun of it. It's when you see sex, murder, and all those things that have an effect in real life—and all treated as if they don't matter. Something is wrong. Making rape casual, making lying casual, making murder casual—what we're doing is screwing around with the moral ecology—and that's wrong. Dead wrong!"

Alan was like Don Quixote, ready to attack any windmill that held a portent of being unfair to any number of people and groups or causes. Still, he sunk his teeth most deeply into the ERA. He was a natural—a popular television star whose private life was apparently as clean as a hound's tooth; a man adored by women, respected, and extremely popular, thanks to "M*A*S*H." Not only was Alan the ideal spokesman, but he went at it with great gusto. Never at a loss for words, now that he was a big star, Alda took the ERA message to the airwaves and the airplanes to reach everybody and anybody within earshot. He created new quotes—slogans that could be picked up and repeated by the rank and file. "The reasonableness of it is so overwhelming," he chirped. "The opposition seems to stem from fear." Alan was roundly cheered and applauded at one fund-raiser when he sounded the death knell, he hoped, for the anti-ERA advocates. "The opposition is not rational to the questions raised. Women who oppose ERA are a puzzle to me. They fear that men will no longer support their wives, that women will be sent into combat, or that housewives will be forced into the work force. Well, what are the realities?" he asks. "There is no draft at the present time and I'm opposed to drafting anybody for war. I feel that when all citizens face a draft, all will take a look at it and resist it."

Alan threw not only himself into this melee for the ERA, but also his family. He and his daughter Elizabeth marched on behalf of the amendment in Tallahassee, the capital of Florida. Leaders of women's rights, such as Gloria Steinem, were certain that Alda would be able to sway the male legislators who wouldn't budge an inch for a female lobbyist.

Times change and so do the programs we grow accustomed to watching. In 1975, while "M*A*S*H" was on the ascent, one of the longest-running series in television history, "Gunsmoke," was canceled. This was indicative of the changing times. There were other changes in the wind. The country was in a recession, and Alan saw that as a reason to pitch men from another angle. His comment was interesting considering his statements on women not being forced into the work market. Speaking on ABC's "Issues and Answers," he noted, "There are a lot of men who are out of work, who would love to see their wives working full time and getting equal pay with other men who might be working in similar jobs."

Alan became chairman of Men for ERA and testified before the Illinois Senate Executive Committee considering the fate of the amendment in that state. "You don't have to be a benevolent emancipator to see women really get an equal place in society. You just have to stand aside." The committee did not stand aside, and never did thereafter. They voted 11 to 8 not to send the proposal to the Illinois Senate floor. It was a tremendous personal loss for Alan, since he had put much effort and time into persuading the august committee that his position was the right one.

That defeat did not end Alan's dedication to the cause. One would have thought he couldn't possibly have the time to be so politically involved with all of the writing, acting, and directing chores he had taken on, but before the year was out, he made his voice heard louder and clearer than ever on the subject of ERA. "Outside of writing and acting," he declared, "the major part of my time is spent in the common effort to see that the ERA becomes law." Opponents, he reasoned, were ill-informed. They didn't understand what ERA was all about. "It's outrageous," he argued, "to think that two hundred years after the founding of the country we're still debating putting a sentence in the Constitution saying women are equal. People who say we don't need it aren't accurately stating the case. I want it in writing!" He was incensed with what he saw as "this so-called protection women enjoy." It was not enough, he stated emphatically. "A scrap of food on the table and a cot in the corner. The husband can live in luxury and throw the wife a bone in the corner and still live within the law." Despite his rhetoric, nobody could doubt Alan's sincerity. He knew from the beginning that he was involved in a movement to break through new frontiers. "As with any new movement," he admitted, "it must include an advance guard whose job is to be tasteless. You have to get everybody's attention."

He was beginning to practice more and more on a daily basis the beliefs about women that he had so eloquently been preaching to legislators. One writer described his marriage at the time as "liberated these days." Arlene was back to her career in music, his family spent their summers with him in Hollywood while maintaining their home in New Jersey, and Alan expressed a desire that we all "accept our responsibility for other people. This is part of the humanism of the movement."

A side of Alan expressed itself vividly through his involvement in ERA—a human understanding of women that most men never even think about. Whether one likes Alan Alda or not, through him much that is good in American women was brought to the forefront. He didn't exclude himself from the .common horde of man he was trying to reach. "We men need to be retrained," he said, "because we have been taught to appreciate superficial qualities in women. We're expected to marry women with exaggerated secondary sex characteristics, and we do, and when we find we're married to an empty person we get outraged. We don't understand it and we go out and look for someone who's exactly the same. It's the person underneath that counts. We need to humanize our responses to each other. They don't realize they're killing themselves. Real food tastes a lot better than sugar-coated, once you get used to it.

"My own marriage began on a traditional note, but has never been superficial. My wife gave up her career to raise our three daughters. We simply did not want to hand our children over to others to raise. We did what we thought was best for the family. We took it for granted that my career was the one we were going to drop everything for. A very significant difference—I don't think we'd make that decision now. It would have taken a few years longer for me, that's all, and she would be further along. You simply cannot rewrite the past. Regrets are useless. They don't get you anywhere."

He felt, he said, that the ERA would not solve all problems between man and woman. "It offers us a new struggle. Marriage will require more work, but you have to work on a marriage anyway if it's going to survive. I don't think work is equivalent to destruction."

Alan sacrificed some of his precious privacy for the ERA. The cause he was espousing of necessity opened up his own personal situation. It was unavoidable, and I'm sure he was often uncomfortable with the questions that were thrown at him by antifeminists. Still his "Mr. Nice Guy" image generally prevailed—an impression he doesn't find at all embarrassing. "Nice guy," he says, "to some means softy, not aggressive. I'm an aggressive person and I fight for the things I believe in. I'm deliberate and jealous of my privacy. I know people want something personal. I figure that's their problem. I'm not Mr. Nice Guy about that. I don't feel I have to be."

CHAPTER 13

When the Federal Communications Commission decreed that violence and adult themes must be eliminated in early-evening prime-time viewing, it created what popularly became known as television's "family hour." Most television executives were not pleased, especially those presiding over the three major networks, ABC, NBC, and CBS. When push came to shove and the industry felt that the FCC had overstepped its authority, fireworks began to pop and crackle.

Finally, the three most powerful trade unions in the entertainment industry, the Screen Actor's Guild, Writers Guild, and Directors Guild on October 30, 1975, filed suit against the FCC in federal court. They alleged that the rules for the family hour, which were being enforced by the three major networks at the government's insistence, were in violation of the First Amendment of the Constitution and were a product of political coercion. Danny Arnold, producer of "Barney Miller" for ABC, alleged, "It's censorship by fear."

Although the networks were no more happy with the concept than the creative forces who provided them with product, they went along with the FCC, fearing even more stringent restrictions if they did not. Consequently, the three major networks were also named in the lawsuit. During a press conference to announce the filing of action, a number of leading television personalities appeared to complain that the FCC had pressured the networks to impose the family hour and had only succeeded in intimidating the networks so that original thought vanished during the 7:00 to 9:00 p.m. time slot, while actually contributing to the increase in violent situations during the later time segments.

It was the first time ever that the three major unions had agreed on a common cause. Among those participating in the news conference were Norman Lear (producer of such controversial shows as "All in the Family" and "Maude"), Carroll O'Connor, Hal Linden, Mary Tyler Moore, and Alan Alda. Mr. O'Connor, the irascible Archie Bunker of "All in the Family," said, "The central issue is not how many 'hells' and 'damns' we used during any of the program, but how the regulation has infringed on the constitutional guarantees of free expression." Alan Alda had a multiple interest in the lawsuit, being a dues-paying member of all three unions.

Meanwhile, "M*A*S*H" was gearing up for a new season. There was much talk about Alan's conciliatory disposition and even temperament. Loretta Swit laughingly disagreed. "Alan isn't even-tempered at all. If you want to see him angry, let him see someone being ill-treated. His emotions get to him. I've seen him cry when he read a letter from one of his daughters. His peace is of an inner variety, which allows him to always be in control of any situation. You have to like yourself first, and Alan does more than that—he respects himself, which in turn allows him to respect others." Loretta had good reason to praise him. Once, at an Equal Rights Amendment affair, he realized that she was the only woman present and urged her to stand up and say so. She was intimidated by all the males in attendance, but he insisted. "He made me feel better about myself. It was a hard thing for me to do. I, like other women, was taught not to pose a threat to men. But I did it and I felt good. I've learned a lot from Alan Alda—about my own sex."

During an interview with Joe Bell from *Good Housekeeping*, Alan revealed, "It's a weird existence, isn't it? I suppose I've learned how to compartmentalize my life, to shift from total concentration on one thing to total concentration on another without losing a beat. But to me, work is love. Work is the heart of health." His fear of anonymity was reflected when he said, "These days we all have a sense of powerlessness because anonymous people are deciding our existence. I'd like to see people in direct contact with those who make basic decisions that affect their lives. ... I think the breakdown of the community *idea* is a great pity. If we bring up a generation of kids without real human contact, they're going to develop like those neurotic monkeys that have been separated from their parents in laboratory experiments. That's happening today, and it worries me a lot."

The last season with the original cast intact showed the following statistics:

Writers:

> *Larry Gelbart (9); Lawrence Marks (6); Everett Greenbaum and Jim Fritzell (6); Linda Bloodworth and Mary Kay Place (2); Sid Dorfman (2); John Regier (1); Gary Markowitz (1); John D. Hess (1); Robert Klane (1); Simon Muntner (1); Arthur Julian (1). Some of these writers co-wrote with Larry Gelbart. Directors: Hy Averback (11); Don Weis (3); Gene Reynolds (4); Lee Philips (1); William Jurgenson (1); and Alan Alda (1).*

There were 110 male and 33 female guest stars. Behind the camera only Linda Bloodworth and Mary Kay Place appeared as writers in two segments. It was the first time that Alan's father, Robert Alda, appeared in a guest stint. Jamie Farr as well as William Christopher, both of whom would eventually become regulars (Farr in season four and Christopher in season five), appeared numerous times. Their popularity made them logical favorites to replace the exiting cast members.

Like the casting changes, there was a lot of fun and games on the "M*A*S*H" set. There seemed to be a running chess game with actors replacing one another as they waited to be called on the set for a scene. Season four inaugurated new faces Mike Farrell and Jamie Farr (who was not a new face, just a new regular). There was another change in

"M*A*S*H." During the 1975-1976 season, the show moved from its old time slot to a new one—Tuesday nights at nine, *after* the so-called family hour. Alan was in an excellent position to express his feelings, having just won another Emmy as outstanding actor in a comedy series.

Somewhat outraged at the government's family hour "nonsense" as so many called it, Alda attacked the proposition with his usual zest. He argued that the government's attempt to curb violence had merely increased it. "We're not even getting a good grade of violence," he argued. "Asking for good violence is like the parent of summer camp complaining about the food. 'You're feeding my son poison here. And in such small quantities.'" Alan saw two kinds of violence being projected: felt violence and unfelt violence. "Unfelt violence is the junk we get all of the time. People being killed, maimed, and brutalized with nobody seeming to feel any of it either physically or emotionally. Not the killers, not the victims—not even their friends." The nightly carnage following the family hour was described by Alan as an "electronic Circus Maximus."

Felt violence, he explained, was something else again. That was the reality of the everyday life we all experience—a violence that left bruises and pain for days or months or even killed, leaving friends and family with heartbreak and grief that often never went away. Even in Shakespeare, he contended, "we are allowed to share the pain and anguish," while on television we look for the bloody tag lines with some glee. The FCC and the networks weren't interested in a dialogue with the creative people in the industry. They resolved the problem by fiat with little or no regard for those responsible for injecting humanity into television fare, that is, actors, writers, and directors.

One of Alan's contemporaries made the most indicting statement against not only the government and the networks but our entire moral fabric when he uttered these words: "One act of love is rated 'X,' while violence in abundance gets a 'PG' nod."

Alan felt that all parents should be concerned about "wanton violence and tasteless humor" on television, but that they should be even more outraged at "censorship" in any form. "It's no laughing matter when they take our jokes away," he anguished. "It is a form of violence that is keenly felt." He succeeded in putting pressure on the network executives, many of whom privately agreed with him but didn't want to put up too much of an argument with the FCC for fear they might find fault with other areas of the giant communications corporations. The family hour concept eventually was recognized to be a failure, and although the FCC has kept a somewhat cautious hand on the throttle, much of the violence has crept back into the seven-to-nine time slot. The government regulatory agencies have had a much greater problem with the onslaught of private cable television, pay television, and satellites.

Alan found things that pleased him, however, both on the "M*A*S*H" set and in his private life. Any thoughts of guilt that he might have harbored because of Arlene's subjugation in their marriage certainly were eased now that she was busy with her own projects, which took her not only into downtown Leonia but all over the country. A truly professional photographer now, she traveled with camera and clarinet. Her proud husband found subjects for her to photograph. For example, he suggested that she be the one to take official pictures of Gary Burghoff's new baby. "You'll get shots," he assured her, "that no one else will be able to get."

His daughters were stretching into lives of their own with school and friends and outside activities. The Alda household was maturing gracefully. Arlene said, "I think we've managed rather well to take care of conflicts in our various schedules—both Alan and myself. We realize that each of us has a need to do something that fulfills an inner demand, just as the girls do." The challenge was to satisfy all their needs without anyone feeling hurt or left out. Alan saw that as no problem because he believed a loving family that can sit down and reason things out together will automatically consider the other's feelings in decision-making situations. "For Arlene and myself," he admitted, "it means that we must simply be ourselves, and that allows a risk to the relationship. We have more going for us than perhaps others because we are not only husband and wife but true friends." Still, he concedes that it is a never-ending task to keep equality and contentment when five individuals are involved.

To learn things, Alan philosophized, you must live them. Experience them. He plays "theater games" continuously—at home, on the set, or at an ERA conference. "I learned from Viola Spolin, an acting teacher, to heighten my awareness by observing what those around me are doing." He applies that to his own family with the idea that living together is the best way to have a keen awareness of one another.

Their marriage had never been stronger, but both were equally adamant in their assessment that each was vulnerable and that each had special strengths to deal with that vulnerability as individuals.

Alan's awareness was of great assistance on the set of "M*A*S*H." His confidence rubbed off on others. For instance, one week when the producers of the show were sweating out ulcers as the Nielsen ratings showed them number forty for the week in standings, Alan was laughing it off, engaging in a game of scrabble with Loretta Swit and Gary Burghoff. Larry Gelbart was widely quoted as being fed up with television and saying he would "return to movies," where sensibility ruled. Alan never took that seriously. He was sure the show would bounce back, and it did. The following week it jumped up to number twenty-three. A pinball machine was brought onto the sound stage, which helped the actors relax even more. Alan simply didn't think all the games the networks and Fox executives played were worth losing sleep or tempers over, and in the final results he was right.

Replacing stars on a successful series is always a dangerous effect. Would the audiences adopt the new characters? That was an intangible that could, hopefully, be resolved positively if everyone cooperated and successors could be found who could slowly be worked into the show without any sudden shock syndrome. Bringing Jamie Farr on as a regular was easy. Fan-mail response to his "drag" character, Corporal Max Klinger, was overwhelmingly in favor of the comic relief within an often absurd situation. The exception was a couple of militant gay groups who felt Klinger's role was a put-down of gays, although Klinger was never supposed to be gay in the role, just a shrewd street kid looking for a way out of the military he detested.

Wayne Rogers' role was by far the most difficult to substitute. McLean Stevenson, the all-too-casual company commander, presented the least problem. He could not be duplicated, nor did the producers think it would be wise to do that. Whoever replaced him would have to carry on administrative duties and still hover like a worried parent over a wounded kid on the operating table. Henry Morgan, who had for many years been one of the outstanding supporting-role actors in both television and motion pictures, was already being considered for the part. A year earlier he came to the attention of the producers when he appeared in a segment as a somewhat uncertain general bent on inspecting the "M*A*S*H" hospital who totally flips out during the tour. Gene Reynolds and Larry Gelbart were united in their belief that Morgan was the only one who should become the new commanding officer.

Morgan, a seasoned veteran, agreed to do the role and his new rank of colonel was never explained. His career went all the way back to an appearance with Henry Fonda in the classic *The Ox-Bow Incident*, right on into television as Jack Webb's deadpan partner in "Dragnet," on from there to the "Pete and Gladys" comedy, playing Pete to Cara Williams' Gladys after a stint on "December Bride."

Loretta Swit expressed the feelings of not only herself but several members of the "M*A*S*H" cast when Farrell and Morgan showed up for rehearsals to begin the fourth season of the show. She explained their dilemma in an interview with Bill Davidson of *TV Guide*: "I approached this season with trepidation bordering on hysteria. It was like being part of a family for three years and then you're told, 'This isn't your brother. *This* guy is your brother.' But the very first day, I realized we had acquired two kindred spirits who would fit into our group just beautifully. Overnight, it was a *new* family."

Alan Alda could not have handpicked anyone more suited in temperament to play opposite him than Mike Farrell. Perhaps he did handpick him, although when Farrell was interviewed as a possible replacement for Wayne Rogers, he was under long-term contract to Universal, an insignificant factor for those concerned. The most important question to the "M*A*S*H" producers was, How would Farrell play against Alda?

Mike was not the only one tested; others were also tested with Alda to see whose chemistry best matched that of Alan. For who knows how much or what concessions, Universal agreed to give Farrell his release. Alan and the producers all agreed—Mike Farrell was the right one to take over the "new doctor" role. As it turned out, Farrell in real life was very much like the B. J. Hunnicutt character he would portray on "M*A*S*H."

Never were two people more suited to work together. Even their "opposite" characteristics attracted them to each other. Whereas Alan had many advantages because of his famous movie-star father, Mike's dad was a movie studio carpenter. Farrell attended Hollywood High School, which he followed with dramatic arts studies at Los Angeles City College and UCLA, the more conventional route to seeking a career in film for those not born to the "purple." A former marine, he became a liberal activist and ecological champion. Like Alan, he was a literate man who had delved deeply into books for knowledge and wisdom. From the very beginning, he became Alan's "buddy" on the "M*A*S*H" set. They not only worked well together but campaigned for causes together. It was as if Alan had found a brother to whom he could relate.

Taking Mike Farrell under his wing, Alan walked with him through the brushy mountain country of their Malibu Canyon exterior location site, and they sat down and between them put together a chessboard comprised of stones on Alan's side of the board and empty beer cans for Farrell. Like two young men feeling each other out they played. Alan, the king of the walk, welcoming the new kid on the block.

Farrell beat him at chess and established his right as an equal. There was no gloating, just a better player beating a good player; they've been close friends ever since.

Larry Linville welcomed Morgan and Farrell to the show. He believed that new faces with new ideas would help spruce up the series and keep everybody on their toes. "How many shows," he asks, "can lose two central figures and continue to get big ratings? Not many—few if any." But "M*A*S*H" did.

In four years, "M*A*S*H" was shifted from day to day and time to time during the week. The first year the opposition on Sunday nights had been "Walt Disney Presents" and "The FBI"; then, the program slipped into the gap between "All in the Family" and "The Mary Tyler Moore Show" on Saturday nights which increased viewers and enabled the infant series to stand up and walk on its own legs. The following year, the show stood alone on Tuesday nights, not an old and seasoned vehicle, but robust enough to compete with the opposition. Still, the CBS network juggled its schedule, trying to out rate rivals NBC and ABC on Friday night, so "M*A*S*H" was literally thrown to the lions and tigers, having to compete with some of the top shows the other networks had to offer: NBC's "Sanford and Son,"

"Chico and the Man,"

"The Rockford Files," and "Police Woman." It was a situation of having to start all over again for recognition. The Friday night viewers on the other channels had a fast- paced lineup, meaning that viewers migrated from one show to the next without touching their dials.

Again, while the producers were pulling out what hair they had left, the actors took it all in stride with an almost Pollyannaish attitude that said, "Something good will happen eventually, so not to worry." And they didn't. Alan's solution to their problem was simple. "What we have to do," he suggested, "is just what we are doing." Eventually, he felt, the network would get smart and either find a better time slot or give the show a better lead-in than "Big Eddie," which then preceded it.

CBS did do something and the "M* A*S*H" bunch almost strangled when they were told the new plans. They announced in November that "M*A*S*H" was going back to Tuesday evening at 9:00 p.m. with a tepid lead-in show called "Joe and Son" and would be pitted against two of the most popular current shows on the tube: ABC's "The Rookies" and the NBC blockbuster starring Angie Dickinson, "Police Woman." The groans from "M*A*S*H," both at the production office level and down on the set, could probably have been heard in Korea. Nobody was pleased and tempers flared and snapped.

Little did anyone know that CBS, for a change, had made the right decision. On December 9, "M*A*S*H" was number one for the week with a forty-two rating share, while "The Rookies" drew a lukewarm twenty-eight. Certainly Alan Alda had something to do with the following the show picked up, but not all. The series itself sustained a certain number of viewers, but I believe it was the addition of new characters and the producers' willingness to make changes and innovations that kept the audience once they were convinced to switch the dial to CBS. Each character developed a following, and none has ever been more popular than Jamie Farr's. The very idea that he could suggest a bit of transvestite spice to the situation became a very human element on a show that dealt with serious matters on a week-to-week basis. So captivated did the viewing audience become with that aspect of his character that when he makes public appearances for a charity or with his nightclub act, it is almost demanded that he include the drag numbers that made him so popular on "M*A*S*H" (and which he will probably incorporate in his new series).

His wife, Joy, thinks it is hilarious that women fawn over him with a Carmen Miranda fruit-laden hat or an outfit all "foo foo" and filled with feathers. "Those women go crazy for me," Farr laughs. "They run to me at airports or wherever and kiss me." What man wouldn't enjoy all that female attention? "One woman stopped nursing her baby merely to get my autograph." In his hometown, Toledo, Ohio, he was once trapped into a situation and signed seven hundred autographs before he could be extracted from the mob of women fans who surrounded him.

Jamie accepts it all quite philosophically. "Who wouldn't love it?" he asks. "After so many years of being just another anonymous face in the crowd. Still"—he grins impishly—"it's a real drag carrying all those hatboxes through airport terminals and hotel lobbies."

During the winter of 1975-1976 Loretta Swit, on hiatus from "M*A*S*H," replaced Ellen Burstyn in the Broadway production of *Same Time, Next Year* (later to become one of Alan's starring films with Ellen Burstyn in the female lead). She had an opportunity then to reflect on herself and her role in "M*A*S*H."

"It is only a role," she said, "and I could never even begin to think of myself as the Hot Lips Houlihan type. I'll always be that chubby ugly duckling from Passaic." Even plastic surgery, she thought, can't change a person from what she really is. "I read a book by one of those guys," she said, "and he said that even after they'd been through all of that, the strange eyes or ears or nose or other peculiarity that characterized that person was still there—the women still saw those flaws in their mind's eye." Similarly, "M*A*S*H" had had its face-lift, but the public still saw the basic structure under the new tucks and stitches.

Gary Burghoff prepared himself for the new season by getting out of town and listening to what people away from Hollywood were saying about "M* A*S*H" and, in particular, his own character. He also talked to reporters and media representatives from radio and television. Someone asked him how he felt about being called "cute." With a boyish grin, he responded, "Aw, I know I'm cute." He then let loose with a blast of rhetoric about cute. "Cute, cute, *CUTE!* I was always cute, because I was always the smallest kid on the block. *I HATE CUTE!*"

He appeared to be surprised that he was recognized parading through a hotel lobby in a smart denim jump suit. "I can't understand it," he scratched his head. "I got rid of my two-day beard and the knit Radar cap, funny glasses, and army fatigues." Being instantly recognized is raw evidence of the popularity of "M*A*S*H."

At the time he was appearing at the Blue Max nightclub in Chicago. Burghoff, like other members of the "M*A*S*H" cast, worked the hustings during the offseason. He is multi-talented. "I do everything," he said. "I sing, I dance, I act—and I do it all very well." He has one gigantic hang-up: He doesn't like to be referred to as "small."

"I don't think five feet six is all *that* short." He has never forgiven singer/comedian Dean Martin for a comment Gary calls "a cheap shot." When Dean had his own show, he had Gary on as a guest. By way of introducing Burghoff, he said: "Well, Gary Burghoff's so small he drives the dog food commercial stagecoach." Gary didn't like it and said so. "I was really hurt when he said that. I'm not short. I'm taller than Arte Johnson or Mickey Rooney."

His interpretation of Radar, by his own admission, is a true miracle of creation since he had no military experience. He was deferred from the draft because of a birth defect—his left hand is small and the fingers end below the first joint. He is not shy about that. "It bothered me while I was growing up. I knew it made me different—set me aside from others—made me *special*."

As a teen-ager he tried to hide the defect from girls. "When I had to make a right turn in the car, I always switched hands quickly so my left hand wouldn't go to the top of the steering wheel. I didn't want my dates to see it." At seventeen, he began to realize there was a lot more to Gary Burghoff than his left hand. From then on, he almost went out of his way to make sure that his dates saw the imperfection. Once he discovered that it didn't matter, he had surmounted probably the biggest mental handicap of his young life. "It certainly doesn't bother me anymore at all," he reveals, holding it up for emphasis. "I learned that if you *think* you are virile, sexy, and attractive, you *are* virile, sexy, and attractive." His philosophy parallels that of Loretta Swit, which may have much to do with the positive statements made by "M*A*S*H."

Each member of the "M*A*S*H" cast found a way to relax and get away from the daily grind of a series during the periods of time when the show was between seasons— Alan, through his wicked sense of humor. He has learned to deal with the reality that he and Arlene are considered "Mr. and Mrs. Ideal Married Couple," and is only amused when anyone assumed that they have never had an argument or disagreement, or that they don't still have them. They do and he's the first to admit it. "We take turns being strong," he points out with total candor. "We also takes turns being smart. If we argue about a decision, it is usually decided by compromise. The bottom line is that we both *care*."

Some of their family habits might be considered eccentric by people who expect the very wealthy to have everything done for them. With the Aldas, the contrary is more often true. For instance, Arlene doesn't care to be fussed about in a beauty parlor, so she cuts and styles her own hair. Her clothes come off the rack because she thinks it is silly to spend fabulous sums on frocks. The wives of many less famous stars spend their husbands into oblivion in order to maintain the "star image." Arlene doesn't think that's important, and her husband applauds her sensibility.

Friends and neighbors hold a healthy respect for Arlene Alda. She never tries to upstage them or allow her husband's position in the world to influence how she feels about herself or other people. She is her own person—without Hollywood frills. One friend said of her, "She's not into elegance." When the Aldas host their annual tennis party in Leonia, it is pure Americana: hamburgers and barbecued chicken without the fancy condiments. It has been said of Arlene, "The most important thing to her is the emotional atmosphere."

Alan's sense of humor came to the forefront one year and Arlene was the pleasantly surprised victim. It was Arlene's birthday and they were still living most of their time in Leonia during the off-season. Alan hosted a brunch for his wife, and one guest, who had arrived with a dozen or so suitcases, told the Aldas that he was en route to a business conference out of the country and would have to leave before the day's event was over. Alan said to Arlene, "Come on, honey, let's drive him to the airport." She agreed and when they arrived at the departing gate, Arlene discovered that the only ones going on a trip out of the country were her and Alan, and it wasn't for business. He really took her by surprise when he announced, "We're going to Paris and *not* for business!" For one of the few times in their marriage, Arlene was speechless. He had personally packed the bags of their "friend" with his and Arlene's belongings, having duplicated each and every item in her makeup kit to be sure she had what she would need.

To be a husband, lover, father, actor, writer, director, and caring human being takes tremendous time and dedication. Larry Balmagia, a writer on "M*A*S*H," seemed to sum up all those things Alan is to those who know him most intimately when he commented, "I don't want to make him sound like God, because he's not, but the fact is Alan does the work of five people."

Although Alan took time out to co-produce, direct, and write an NBC comedy special, *Hickey vs. Anybody*, which aired in September 1976, his primary devotion was still to "M*A*S*H." Jack Weston, incidentally, starred in this production about a lawyer attempting to sue the city (typical antiestablishment Alan Alda script). Weston would be remembered when Alan was casting *The Four Seasons* for the wide screen. Alan's father was also at Twentieth Century-Fox that year, appearing in a motion picture that was probably filmed on location in Rome where he was still residing. The film, *I Will I Will ... for Now*, starred Elliott Gould (from the film "M*A*S*H"), Diane Keaton, Paul Sorvino (who had starred in the ill-fated series "We'll Get By," scripted by Alan Alda), and Victoria Principal, now one of the many stars of "Dallas." Bob Alda was billed fifth in the movie, but probably made more money than some of those above him on the credits. The interesting revelation is that so many people who were, from time to time, associated with Alan and his father over the years found themselves as Alan's costars in both television and movie productions later on. It says something for Alan's sense of loyalty to those he cares about.

The regulars on the fourth season of "M*A*S*H" were Alan Alda, Gary Burghoff, Larry Linville, Mike Farrell, Harry Morgan, Loretta

Swit, and Jamie Farr. All the shows for the fourth season were produced by Gene Reynolds and Larry Gelbart.

The scripts were produced by:

> Jim Fritzell and Everett Greenbaum (8); Larry Gelbart (4); Simon Muntner (3); Jay Folb (1); Glen Charles and Les Charles (1); Rich Mittleman (1); John D. Hess (1); Burt Prelutsky (2); Linda Bloodworth (1); Gene Reynolds (3); John Regier and Gary Markowitz (1). The shows were directed by: Gene Reynolds (7); John Erman (1); Alan Alda (4); Charles S. Dubin (1); Burt Metcalfe (3); William Jurgensen (2); George Tyne (1); Harry Morgan (1).

In spite of Alan's outings on behalf of the ERA and total equality for women, the so-called weaker sex reached a low ebb in connection with "M*A*S*H." Male guest stars numbered fifty-four, while only nine guest stars were women. There was only one woman in a prominent position behind the camera, Linda Bloodworth.

CHAPTER 14

Having Mike Farrell as a compatriot on the set of "M*A*S*H" eased many of the tensions Alan might have had during the workaday schedule of filming the show. The two hung out together, joking and sharing casually in the manner of two young men growing up together in the carefree environs of a Kansas wheat farm.

During a day when George Vecsey was preparing a story for *Reader's Digest* about "M*A*S*H" and Alan in particular, he observed the following: As both Alda and Farrell were lounging about waiting to be called on the set to do a scene, Mike spotted a unicycle leaning against the wall. He ambled, on legs like bowed stilts, over to the bike and attempted a ten-second spin, which distracted Alan, who was before the cameras busily flubbing his lines. Each time he tried to repeat the elusive line, he would break up with a loud-pitched cackle, which created a similar response from the other actors in the scene. Just when it appeared that the scene would never be properly shot, Alan shouted to one and all: "That's all right. I don't want anybody to know I'm in this scene anyway." Having Farrell around did that to Alan.

On the set Alan might clown around with Mike Farrell, but away from filming "M*A*S*H," he was another kind of person. More and more, he was expounding the inequalities of women in America. Discarding his surgeon's garb and dressed in the respectable business suit of a big hospital doctor, he addressed a nurses' convention in Atlantic City, with a message that endeared him to the feminists there. Doctors, he contended, consider nurses little more than "handmaids" because of the stereotype that women are inferior to men. "You could eliminate sexism in your jobs," he preached, "by supporting the ERA." At that time, the amendment was still four states short of ratification. "What we need," he continued, "is a clear signal to the courts on sex like we had on race, that this is something the country has said is wrong."

At this point in his multifaceted career, Alan was aware that he was no ordinary run of the mill star. Thanks to "M*A*S*H" he was now in the superstar category. His response to a woman's inquiry of a national magazine as to when he first felt he was making it in show business is indicative of his confidence in just who he was. "The obvious answer is when my press interviews started picking up. I figured if people wanted to read about me, then I was starting to make a name for myself. But on a more domestic level, I felt secure when I realized I'd reached the point where I could decently provide for my family." It can be safely stated that when he spoke to the nurses in Atlantic City he was totally ensconced in job security and ready to tackle another year of "M*A*S*H."

While Alan was well into the fifth season of "M*A*S*H," his father was working with Elke Sommer, Telly Savalas, and a large cast of Italian actors in a devilish non-epic, *House of Exorcism*. Father and son kept in close contact with each other, each reading the other's reviews thoughtfully and with a great sense of pride. Alan's popularity may have surpassed that of his elder, but he never made a conscious effort to upstage his father. Respect was the most important quality implanted in Alan's personality by his parents—particularly respect for father.

Alan came in for his share of respect early in 1977 when Gary Deeb, the TV-radio critic for the *Chicago Tribune*, made him the subject of his column. Deeb's columns, often written with what appears to be hemlock for ink, are feared and revered by television personalities. He has always detested Hollywood personalities who capitalize on their charity and fund-raising appearances. He refers to Danny Thomas's pitches as "transforming the 'Tonight Show' into a communion breakfast." He has a list of pompous entertainers who are "consumed by an inflated idea of their own importance." Among those included in his "Pompous Sweepstakes" are Jerry Lewis, Carroll O'Connor, Marlon Brando, Shirley MacLaine, Jack Lemmon, Howard Cosell, and Sammy Davis, Jr., whom Deeb refers to as "the man who hugged Richard Nixon."

You won't find Alan Alda's name on any of Deeb's obnoxious lists. He refers to Alan as "a rare performer who truly cares about the world he lives in, who can articulate his feelings with compassion and humility, and who generates absolutely no pretension."

That was just the lead-in to a rave critique of Alan's performance in the role of Caryl Chessman, a California rapist who was executed in the San Quentin gas chamber after a record twelve years on death row. The movie made for television, *Kill Me if You Can,* brought praise for Alan equal to that he received for his brilliant performance in Truman Capote's *The Glass House.*

During his interview with Deeb, Alan covered as many topics as possible. Opposed to the death penalty, Alan expressed his anguish over the Utah execution of Gary Gilmore by a firing squad the day before. "Our society," he said, "through capital punishment is encouraging more people to murder." He theorized that the state was actually telling people it is okay to "snuff" a person out if you hate them enough. The only good thing about the death penalty, he said, is the feeling of revenge we get once the deed is done. "Capital punishment isn't a deterrent to crime," he declared, "but actually an inducement to murder."

Hollywood is a world unto itself where "style" and "image" comprise the better part of public relations. Deeb said of Alda's projections, "It's a refreshing style that ought to become an 'in' thing. Then the rest of Hollywood would adopt it in no time." Maybe. Hollywood has a history of faddism.

During the "M*A*S*H" hiatus in 1977, Alan took time out to write a thirty-minute comedy special for NBC, coproduced also by Alan with Mark Merson. Entitled "Susan and Sam," the cast included Christine Belford as Susan, Robert Foxworth (now starring in "Falcon's Crest"), and Lee Bergere (the pseudoaristocratic houseman on "Dynasty"). Alan's writing plaudits were quite credible. He also guest-stinted on "CBS Galaxy," a sixty-minute music-comedy-variety special with a format similar to the Colgate comedy specials of the fifties. The guest list read like a *Who's Who* of CBS.

For a man who publicly demands that his privacy be respected, he is a constant source of controversy. He cannot deny that his opinions on issues do not reveal the private Alan Alda, otherwise one has to accept a thesis that says Alan Alda is all public when he deals with ERA or the death penalty. Those firm convictions come from the deepest roots of the private Alan Alda.

Friends have leaked tidbits from the inner sanctum of the Alda home castle. Mario Thomas, a close personal friend of the Aldas, discussed their relationship with their three daughters, observing that the Aldas have never treated their children like "little kiddies." She implied that the children had rights equivalent to those of adults, although they have never publicly exerted those rights because Alan has, along with Arlene, prevailed in his right as a parent to keep them out of the public eye.

Alan, I believe, was speaking from deep emotion when he said, "I feel sometimes I'm getting the short end of it because I need them more than they need me." Alan has said over and over again that it was Arlene who had the responsibility of the young girls while he looked for work during the early years of their marriage. Yet after he became a success with "M*A*S*H" and was busy espousing the rights of women, he declared that with their first child, he had, for years, in addition to diapering and feeding her, washed her diapers out in the cold water of the bathroom toilet bowl. This was during a period when Alan was coming out of the Cleveland Playhouse and working in New York in off-Broadway productions as well as working in parts on various television shows emanating out of New York as well as Hollywood. This late description of his living accommodations sounds more like Spanish Harlem than midtown Manhattan.

Still, there is a ferocious loyalty on the part of friends and associates. Mario Thomas declares that he is so fair he "ought to be a judge" and that one need never be suspicious of his motives. Representative Margaret Hochler, Alan's co-chairman on the Presidental Equal Rights subcommittee, spoke in warm terms when asked about Alan. She thought him sensational and one of the ERA's most "potent forces." She admired his enlightenment and suggested that "committed men like Alan Alda are essential" to the equal rights movement.

"M*A*S*H" continued to be a base of Alan's visibility, so important to the causes he espoused and to which he so sparingly lent his name (only those causes he truly believed in). Alan once told a friend that he would drop "everything" to go anywhere at any time to help promote the ERA.

Regulars on "M*A*S*H" during the fifth season were Alan Alda, Gary Burghoff, Larry Linville, Mike Farrell, Harry Morgan, Loretta Swit, Jamie Farr, and newcomer William Christopher. Bill Christopher was new as a regular, but not a new face on the show. He had appeared in numerous segments during prior seasons of the show. In the beginning, it had been thought that Father Mulcahy, Christopher's role, would be a running regular. It was not until the fifth season, however, that he was officially credited as a regular member of the "M*A*S*H" cast. His presence factored largely in projecting to the viewing audience that people at war have spiritual and emotional problems and that they also *die*. The United States is essentially a religious (particularly Christian) nation. Mulcahy represented the moral side of the American society amid the boozing, womanizing tendencies toward immorality that prevailed on "M*A*S*H." He was that stablizing character who seemed to stand in the doorway of the embalming room and say, "We don't laugh over a corpse."

The executive producer for the fifth season was Gene Reynolds. Producers were Don Reo, Alan Katz, and Burt Metcalfe. Directors were:

> *Gene Reynolds (7); Alan Alda (4); Burt Metcalfe (5); Alan Rafkin (2); Joan Darling (1); George Tyne (1); William*

Jurgensen (2); Harry Morgan (1); Joshua Shelley (1). Writers for the fifth season: Jim Fritzwell and Everett Greenbaum (5); Gary Markowitz (1); Burt Prelutsky (3); Alan Katz and Don Reo (1); Linda Bloodworth (1); Alan Alda (2); Richard Cogan (1); Gene Reynolds and Jay Folb (2); Bill Idelson (1); Jay Folb (1); John D. Hess (1); Sid Dorfman (1); Ken Levine and David Isaacs (2); Gene Reynolds (1); Gene Reynolds, Don Reo Alan Katz, and Jay Folb (1).

In the role of guest star, there were seventy-four male and thirty-eight female actors. The ratio was up for women in front of the camera. It was the first season in which a woman director, Joan Darling, was used, directing from a script by Linda Bloodworth (who had previously written with Mary Kay Place). Two actors with names that are well known to television viewers—Gregory Harrison (now starring in "Trapper John") and Larry Wilcox (starring in "CHIPS")—were also featured.

Statistically, through five seasons of "M*A*S*H" there were 372 male guest stars and 157 female ones. Behind the camera, during the first 120 segments of "M*A*S*H," eight episodes were either written or co-written by women and one show was directed by a woman. Meanwhile, Alan Alda continued to crisscross the country demanding equal rights for women.

During the spring of 1978, Secretary of State Cyrus Vance addressed the 330 graduates of Fordham University Law School, urging them to seek "more innovative approaches to making justice available for all." At that same commencement celebration, Alan Alda was presented an honorary degree, a doctor of fine arts, for his "sense of caring." Alan had a few well-chosen words of wisdom for the eight thousand interested parties assembled. "Politicians," he advised, "can't be bought anymore—that's not to say a few of them can't be rented." That brought a round of applause and an equal amount of guffaws. Television, a medium in which he was an expert, was another subject. "It's one of those unspoken assumptions," he announced seriously, "that violence can be tolerated as long as you ignore it and have no reaction to it." Bringing in another cause, through the back door, he went on to say, "I wonder if there's any connection between the long acceptance by our people of the Vietnam War and the thousands and thousands of deaths we've seen that were never mourned—never even paused for, except to sell shampoo for sixty seconds."

Alan also spoke at the installation dinner of the Hollywood Women's Press Club, continuing to campaign for the ERA. He told the guests and members of the club, especially those in the media, to "implement whatever changes you can through you work," something he was attempting to do on his "M*A*S*H" series. "We've been trying to accumulate some research on nurses. We want to reflect as much as we can on the female experience, and I think we'll find out something about the doctors from those nurses that we haven't found out yet—because sometimes women can tell you things about men that the men are not able to tell you about themselves." Asked why he was so enthusiastic and emotional about obtaining rights for women—a group he wasn't even a member of—he was somewhat at a loss to respond. "I wish I had some dramatic story to tell," he responded. Someone else in the room asked Alda if he thought that having a men's auxiliary (which the Hollywood Women's Press Club had) was sexist. The crowd roared with laughter. Alan did not laugh. He didn't think it was funny. "I'm telling you, sexism is not just impolite. It can be lethal." He went on to explain a delayed answer to the question. "I think," he said, "when you have an oppressed group, they have a right to organize for their betterment. The time will come when we should integrate every group. But I think it would be great for men to go through a period of apprenticeship where *they* find out what it's like to be an auxiliary."

Patsy Meyers, an attorney and wife of Julian Meyers, one of the club's auxiliary male members (and also one of the great publicity men in motion-picture history), commented about Alan's discourses on equal rights. "I'm fully liberated," she stated. "Sometimes I'm auxiliary to my husband, sometimes he's auxiliary to me. We do all the household chores together because I'm a professional. I can't tell you what it's like to live in a house where two parties are equal. I would hope that for everyone."

Continuing his life of high visibility, Alan did guest shots on a number of television shows, including another of those CBS "let us show you our talent" specials. "CBS: On the Air," hosted by Mary Tyler Moore and Walter Cronkite, was not the usual special. It was a nine-and-a-half-hour extravaganza of music, comedy, and variety acts that featured Alan on a Tuesday night along with Gary Moore and Phil Silvers. CBS stars of past, present, and future were paraded before prime-time audiences over a period of one week. It was like a pre-Easter special. Meanwhile, Robert Alda was appearing as a Roman pope in the Italian film *Cagliostro*, continuing to remain in Rome, where Flora's health was back to normal and they were beginning to contemplate a return to the United States to settle down, probably in California.

Having won an Emmy for directing a recent episode of "M*A*S*H," Alan began to publicly espouse his theories on Hollywood and, more particularly, Hollywood motion pictures. In a piece he did for a national news magazine, he commented on the new genre of movies and the new sophistication of audiences as compared to audiences of the thirties. Movies, he said, "are getting a little more human." More what real life is, he explained, citing such films as *Julia* and *The Goodbye Girl* as "wonderful movies." He also plugged his new film, not yet released, *Same Time, Next Year.* "It's about a man and woman people can identify with."

Contending that he did not push for "naughty" words in television, he nonetheless felt that one should be able to represent people as they really talk.

Speaking of the antiwar message of "M*A*S*H," Alan declared that "no war has made any sense to me. I'm not even in favor of the American Revolution."

Suddenly, "M*A*S*H" lost one of its parents and guiding lights. After five years of nursing and baby-sitting scripts and actors, Larry Gelbart voluntarily left the production to do other things. His departure strengthened Alan's control over the show. One critic-writer observed that Alan's only weakness was "his tendency toward sermons" in his acting as well as directing and writing. He was, William Henry II noted in a September 1978 issue of *Horizon*, "less interested in the conflict between the individual and authority, it seemed, than in the tension between romanticism and cynicism within each man." Cynicism seemed to be framed in Alan's words when he commented that he was "once more poor than most of the people watching the show." It is difficult to understand if he was speaking in generalities or specifics.

Alan admits that he knows nothing about the life of migrant workers, but has a working familiarity with the lower middle class. "You don't necessarily feel all that secure because you have money." Most actors would give him a hearty *Amen* to that statement because most actors are notoriously insecure.

The American Women in Radio and Television awarded Alan their 1978 Silver Satellite Award. Alan, on location in Maryland shooting *The Seduction of Joe Tynan*, was unable to receive the award in person. "M*A*S*H" buddy Mike Farrell accepted the trophy, citing Alda as "pure genius," adding that "he is not only the actor, but the writer, director, producer, and consultant," on "M*A*S*H." Alda sent a wire of acceptance in which he acclaimed "the clear strong voice of women in broadcasting," adding that the industry needed them to "make better decisions than are now being made." TV now, he said, "is being turned into a burlesque house." He added, as a tag line, "In twenty-one years of marriage my wife has turned a male chauvinist pig into a tiger for the ERA."

"M*A*S*H" completed its sixth season. Between the sixth and seventh season, Alan completed three feature-length motion pictures, appeared in several guest shots on television, and made speeches for the ERA and liberalism.

While Alan busied himself with movies and speeches, other members of "M*A*S*H" spread out in various directions on their own. Jamie Farr toured the dinner-theater circuit as the star of *Come Live with Me*, a comedy play. Gary Burghoff was off with his patently popular nightclub act, and Loretta Swit devoted much of her time to painting in watercolors, sketching and adding, as she calls it, to her "collections." Few know that she wrote and illustrated a children's book, is a religiously faithful devotee to Yoga, and plays tennis, her favorite sport.

In addition to acting in three films during the hiatus, Alan also scripted *The Seduction of Joe Tynan*, the reviews of which would come later.

"M*A*S*H" finished its sixth season with the following statistics: Burt Metcalfe was the sole producer for the season. The regular cast:

> *Alan Alda, Gary Burghoff, David Ogden Stiers (who replaced Larry Linville), Mike Farrell, Harry Morgan, Loretta Swit, Jamie Farr, and William Christopher. The season's directors were: Hy Averback (1); Don Weis (4); Alan Alda (4) (Alda also wrote each of the segments he directed); Burt Metcalfe (4) (co-directing one segment with Alda); Charles S. Dubin (4); Harry Morgan (1); George Tyne (3); Stuart Miller (1); William Jurgensen (2). Writers: Jim Fitzell and Everett Greenbaum (5); Alan Alda (4); Burt Prelutsky (3); Bill Idelson (1); Ken Levine and David Isaacs (4); Laurence Marks (2); Larry Balmagia (2); Ronny Graham (2) (one co-written by Graham, Ken Levine, and David Isaacs); Allyn Freemen (1).*

During the season there were eighty-eight male and thirty-five female guest appearances. Men were favored two to one as guests and women were absent in the writing/directing department.

Alan's film, *Same Time, Next Year*, in which he costarred with Ellen Burstyn, was released late in the year and the reviews were mixed at best. One critic said, "This is cozy adultery, between two ciphers who are devoted to each other. I've sensed more physical attraction between two neighbors gossiping across the back fence." He went on to further bury Alda's effort: "If someone you make the mistake of caring about insists on your going to this movie, take a small flashlight and a book." He posed the question, "Didn't Alda recognize that this material is like kapok? It's like wadding for your mind—and Alda is trying to find some truth in it."

Larry Linville was the next to leave "M*A*S*H." If the rumored bitter taste left in his mouth when he exited is any indication of how Alan felt, it's likely Alan found one less irritation. The two of them did not get along. Larry was so upset he refused to even discuss Alan Alda.

With seven seasons of "M*A*S*H" behind him, Alan was probably seeing the light at the end of the tunnel. "M*A*S*H" could not go on forever. It had already outdistanced the Korean War three times and probably had hosted more casualties than several wars. Only two characters remained from the pilot episode outside of Alan Alda. They were Gary Burghoff and Loretta Swit. It was rumored around Hollywood that many of the regulars had left because of Alan. The studio publicity department, of course, always had other stories to the contrary: The actor was tired of the show; greener pastures were ahead, or they wanted to get into other things before they became stereotyped.

Once again, the season was produced totally by Burt Metcalfe. Regulars were Alan Alda, Gary Burghoff, David Ogden Stiers, Mike Farrell, Harry Morgan, Loretta Swit, Jamie Farr, and William Christopher. Stiers' character, Charles Emerson Winchester III, re-placed Larry Linville's Major Frank Burns, the object of Hot Lips Houlihan's frustrated affections. Stiers was another character who pre-pared himself for things to come, having guested several times on the show. That seemed to work on "M*A*S*H"—having actors break in as guest stars and then using them to replace a departing actor.

Directors for the seventh season:

> George Tyne (2); James Sheldon (1); Burt Metcalfe (5); Alan Alda (5); Charles S. Dubin (5); Tony Mordente (2); Mel Damski (1); William Jurgensen (2); Mike Farrell (1); Harry Morgan (1). Morgan was allowed his annual directing chore and Mike Farrell now joined the in-house, acting/directing team. Writers: Ken Levine and David Isaacs (5); Larry

Balmagia (2); Ronny Graham (2); Sheldon Bull (1); Ken Levine, David Isaacs, Larry Balmagia, and Ronny Graham (2); Ken Levine, David Isaccs, and Johnny Bonaduce (1); Tom Reeder (1); Alan Alda (3); Erik Tarloff (1); Larry Balmagia and Bernard Dilbert (1); Mitch Markowitz (2); Burt Metcalfe and Alan Alda (1).

There were no women in either directorial or writer's positions.

In the guest appearance category, there were seventy- two males and thirty-one females (including Mike Farrell's wife, Judy, who appeared in one segment). Nothing much for the feminists to see as exciting news.

More and more, if statistics mean anything at all, it appeared that Alan Alda had multiple talents. There was the one Alan Alda who acted, one who wrote, one who directed (all on "M*A*S*H", where he, not so incidentally, had a great amount of clout). Then there was the Alan Alda who produced, wrote, directed, and acted in motion pictures. There was also the Alan Alda who espoused women's rights, abolition of the death penalty, and other causes. But where was the missing link? The Alan Alda who practiced what he was preaching? In one issue of *People* magazine, a letter to the editor asked: "There's Mr. Ms. doing his ERA thing again. If Alda is so supportive of equal rights for women, then why aren't there any women writers and directors on his TV show, 'M*A*S*H'?"

Alan was permitted to respond: "There have been episodes of "M*A*S*H" written and directed by women, but as in all of TV not enough. The show and the studio have tried to remedy that by offering women the chance in both categories." The odds were better on a nag that ran last in its last outing than for a woman to score as a writer or director on "M*A*S*H." In 169 segments of "M*A*S*H," 8 segments were written by women and one was directed by a woman.

The facts of "M*A*S*H" dispute the glowing praise that Alan has bestowed on what a chauvinist might call "the distaff side."

CHAPTER 15

"In its early years," Alan tells a writer, "'M*A*S*H'" shows involved people playing tricks on each other. Now the characters are taken more seriously. But the basic theme is still about people trying to maintain their sanity in an insane situation, making the best of a place they don't want to be."

The question is raised consistently. Are Alan Alda and Hawkeye Pierce actually the same person? It is a question at which Alan becomes almost tongue-tied. He indicates that he *hopes* the two are total opposites, seeing Hawkeye as a fantasy—perhaps an extension of the secret world of his dreams. "An awful lot of what I do when I play Hawkeye is sort of intuitive," he says, but admits that there is some of Hawkeye in Alan Alda, but only from the point of view that he tries to play the part as if he had Hawkeye's background. Given the right circumstances he says, "I suppose I can be as cynical as Hawkeye gets—even being a smart aleck." But he cautions that that is merely an outlet for his sense of humor and not meant in a negative vein.

Alan believes that he can jump from Hawkeye into any other role without taking that personality with him. "I've played many characters," he informs candidly. "Did you know that I made eight movies before I came onto this series? Of course not. Nobody remembers."

He doesn't believe that his own identity depends on what an actor does as much as the material with which he becomes involved, believing that a movie "succeeds because the whole picture works, not because of the actors in it."

Movie stars appear in big box-office flops and turn right around and emerge, smelling like roses, once they have a big hit. Television actors, Alan admits, have a different situation. In a rare instance of labeling himself as a television product, rather than a movie one, he says, "If a TV star makes a movie flop, it's cause for concern." Although Alan has had flops, to date it hasn't really done him a lot of personal damage because he has always had "M*A*S*H" to fall back on. When he leaves the security of a weekly series, then—and only then—he will be faced with analyzing whether the public was more in love with Hawkeye than with Alan Alda.

Alda, who traversed back and forth across the country between New Jersey and Hollywood for more years than he cares to think about, sacrificed much in the way of family. He was speaking as a man who knows when he said, "The shelf life of a family isn't long." He was making reference to the movie he wrote and starred in, *The Seduction of Joe Tynan*. It is the film most critics believe came about because of Alan's own experiences. There are parallels, of course, but he doesn't admit that much of it is autobiographical. "There is tremendous pressure on all of us to devote ourselves to our work instead of to the people we care the most about." He adds, "Your excuse will always be, 'I'm doing this for them'—if you really wanted to do something for 'them,' you would give them *you*, not your success."

Although his work has preordained that he be "elsewhere" instead of with family most of the time, he doesn't agree that it has always been the right thing to do. One of his top priorities—one of society's, he believes—is to put people first. Especially family. Compromise your integrity and you've lost the whole ball game. Still, he says we all have options. Somehow, in the American dream, it has been indelibly stenciled in the psyche that everyone should be successful regardless of the cost. Alan shakes his head and, recognizing the temptation, a temptation he fell victim to himself, says,

"We don't have to do as everybody else does. What are we going to miss? Money? Plaques to hang on the wall?" He is serious. He wonders how you get through the rest of your life, having accomplished "success," dealing with those you have hurt because you were more concerned with "making it" than with their feelings.

Although Alan was speaking in connection with his motion picture, one starts to wonder if Hawkeye Pierce hasn't created a paradox for himself. On the surface he hates war, yet jokes about it. Underneath he definitely hates it, but the prospect of the war ending and his going home must rattle his psyche.

No movie that Alan has ever participated in and no television project, other than "M*A*S*H," received as much critical notice as *The Seduction of Joe Tynan.* It may be that the critics and public at large hoped to find some key to the real Alan Alda. As we've noted, many writers were reading the private Mr. Alda into the ambitious senator all the way down the line. It is interesting to note some of the comments from the reviews of Alan and the film.

James Lardner, *Washington Post*, wrote:

> *Alan Alda ... has peopled his government with a shallow collection of drunks, make-out artists, mental cases, hatchet persons, and megalomaniacs.*

> *And one of the shabbiest public servants of them all, alas, is the senator played by Alda himself.*

Alan argues that the film is not about the senator's public life, but rather his private life. The question arises, Was Alan taking Alda and placing him in the Washington celebrity merry-go-round as a manner of cleansing the Hollywood Alda? As Lardner points out, "This being Washington ... it should hardly surprise anyone if the political side of the movie, however incidental, comes in for unusually close scrutiny here."

The problem, Lardner suggests, is not the stark context into which its hero is thrown; it is the hero himself, as Alan chose to write and act him. "This telegenic, well-tailored senator from New York doesn't have an idea of his own in the movie." Of Alan's costar, Meryl Streep, he said, "She runs the show as few actresses have since the generation of stars who passed their prime in the 1940s." The Alda script, according to this critic's implications, in a sense castrated the male lead. And this from Alan's own pen!

Even though he is referred to as the "writer" of *Tynan*, Alda did have help from *Washington Post* political writer Richard Cohen, his collaborator. Cohen gave him plenty of inside intelligence regarding the Washington scene. The Alda imprint is there, however, and therefore the critics zeroed in on him rather than his co-writer.

In defense of his script, Alan argued, "What's personal is also political. The way we behave toward each other in our most intimate moments—the way a man and woman treat each other in bed, the way a mother or father behaves toward a child, the way a boss deals with his employees—these are the moments that move history forward. More damage is done in those intimate encounters than has been done in wars." Alan's view of his contemporaries, as a senator, was brutal to the point of making one wonder if what Alan Alda really has is a hard-on for the world—to reduce everyone and everything, except himself, to groveling subservients. He admits that having campaigned for the ERA has caused him to become somewhat "cynical and embittered" toward the political scene and politicians. "I used to campaign for Senator George McGovern and former Senator Eugene McCarthy. I could campaign for an issue now, but I don't know if I could campaign for a candidate. Candidates and officeholders tend to be a collection of appearances rather than people with substance." His appraisal of popular politicians could easily be applied to actors and even to himself—since his image, to most people, is that of the irresponsible character of Hawkeye Pierce.

In one breath he admits to a certain embitteredness and cynicism about politics, and in another he says, "I don't really value cynicism very highly and it's not really a true picture of how I feel."

Nonetheless he is outspoken about his feelings "deep down inside" about politics. "I don't find any excitement in politics ... but you can't get away from it. We live in a political atmosphere.... It's like taking out the garbage. It's something that has to be done."

There were good reviews of *Joe Tynan*. The most glowing offered by Janet Maslin of *The New York Times*. "Mr. Alda offers someone who genuinely cares about his diverse interests, even when they conflict, and who has a natural talent for making sound choices."

Kirk Honeycutt of the *Los Angeles Daily News* gave Alda a no-confidence vote. "The film itself is bloodless," he wrote.

Alda has written a script of conveniences. ... In one very poorly handled sequence (let's blame director Jerry Schatzberg for some of this, too), a fellow senator talks to Tynan about their gradually forgetting why they are in the Senate and this talk continues over a shot of a nearly empty Senate corridor. We really do get the movie's point without the lecture. For all this, the film is frequently engaging, thanks largely to the two actresses (Barbara Harris and Meryl Streep) and Rip Torn.... But it almost appears that Schatzberg shot Alda's first draft.

Newsweek praised Alan personally. The reviewer said in summation,

Now the film career that eluded him in such forgettable movies as *Paper Lion* and *The Extraordinary Seaman* has finally arrived. After an ineffectual performance in *Same Time, Next Year* and a winning one in *California Suite*, Alda's work in *Joe Tynan* should make it clear that his low-key charisma is as effective on the big screen as on the tube.

As an advocate of causes, Alan has found a ready platform anywhere he goes. Anyone with such a "good" image was construed to be someone people would listen to. Consequently, he became much in demand as a speaker—and Alan loves to speak about his beliefs. While being interviewed by Howard Kissel of *Women's Wear Daily* during the summer of 1979, a woman chaperoning a group of girls recendtly graduated from high school came over to his table at Maxwell's Plum. Following her charges—who asked for autographs and were sent away with the usual Alda handshake—she gave his hand the best shaking it had all day and gave him pause to think perhaps an autograph would have been the easier way out. She impressed Alda immediately when she profusely thanked him for his work on behalf of the Equal Rights Amendment. Alda explained to Kissel that he was pleased she "is aware of my efforts on behalf of feminism."

He wanted to make it plain that his wife, Arlene, was not responsible for his interest in campaigning for the ERA. Aware of his high visibility because of his celebrity, he says, "I decided I might be useful, but I'm not endorsing the ERA like soap. I don't want people to vote for it because I'm cute." One of the big things Alda learned campaigning for women's rights is that "people do good for bad reasons, bad for good reasons." The people who make the major decisions that control our lives seem to be "motivated by no values, only what keeps them in money, sex, and power."

He tells the story, without naming names of course, about an Illinois state legislator who told a female lobbyist, during the campaign to get the ERA passed in that state, he would consider voting for the amendment, and then gave her the key to his hotel room. "That," Alda contends, "is like voting for emancipation in exchange for a couple of good slaves."

Being an active feminist, he reveals, has changed his perspective on "entertainment." He explained to Kissel, "The other night we had the TV on, and Buddy Hackett was doing one of those knife-throwing acts with a beautiful girl. It was presented to us as entertainment that a man is shooting knives at a defenseless, attractive woman who, for a few minutes, is in danger of being mutilated by him. What does that arouse in us?" It is an old Alda stereotype of the chauvinistic man, one he has used often when being interviewed. Perhaps one day he will explain what it arouses, rather than asking the question.

Perhaps it was a year in which Alan did too much—the quality of his work having been diluted by its overwhelming quantity. If *Joe Tynan* was the victim of critical darts, *California Suite* was not excepted. Even Neil Simon came in for a drubbing from the critics. One cynical reviewer wrote:

> These WASP plays represent the serious side of Neil Simon, which turns out to be surprisingly close to Noel Coward—not good Coward but mawkishly bittersweet Coward, in which gallant people use bitchy wisecracks to conceal their breaking hearts. In texture and attitude, these plays might be something Simon dug up that was buried in London during the blitz. Alan Alda is too self-conscious. Wearing bangs like a Roman emperor, and with his eyes made up to look bigger and bluer, he has a hangdog look. He gives such a flabby, insecure performance that Bill doesn't seem to be a full person.... Fonda is more than Alda's match ... California Suite would seem to give offense to just about everyone: It goes from confirming the stereotypes of henpecked baggy-pants Jews [to those of] blacks who act like clowning savages. And one could hardly claim that it was well made.

Alan, of course, totally disagreed. "It is some of Neil Simon's best writing. There's a very moving attitude throughout the film about how difficult it is for people to live together. Jane and I in the film really admire each other, but the only way we can remain friends is to stay apart. That's sad."

Actors can be the most boring people in the world, and when they are praising themselves, it can become a study in nausea. Once prodded for something devastating in his private life, he told a writer, "There is nothing. Anyway, I wouldn't tell you if there was—but there isn't. I'm perfect." He did admit that he sometimes eats peas with his fingers, which was quite a concession from a man who fosters the image of "Mr. Good Guy." Someone said of sports counterpart, Steve Garvey, the Los Angeles Dodgers' first baseman, "He's such a goody-goody you wish you had a mirror with his picture on it—then you'd always be flaw-less." Alda's "image" is easily as plastic and slick-surfaced as Garvey's. Things like that don't happen by accident; they are programmed by the highest paid experts in the business, the publicity men who create and maintain images in a town where image is *almost* everything.

The publicists assigned to "M*A*S*H" kept a low profile on some aspects of the show. "M*A*S*H," with all its popularity, wasn't per-formed before an audience. Therefore, all of the guffaws and on-cue laughter came from a laugh track. Very few know that because it was a well-kept secret. Somehow or other, a phony laugh track at just the right time takes away from the spontaneity of any comedy show. Alan was always aware of that. Critics dislike it and say so. One remarked that you watch the scene, set in 1950 Korea, and suddenly you hear a Hollywood audience laughing.

Alan appeared to enjoy that anguish. "Yes, and it's taken them twenty-nine years to get the joke. I hate it, too, as does everybody else on the show." He hates it less, he says, than he used to because he be-lieves the actors have been able to circumvent much of it. "We've had serious shows without laugh tracks that have worked." He points out that "M*A*S*H" plays all over the world—Mexico, England—without laugh tracks, "and it's still very popular without them." Alan blames the networks for insisting on laugh tracks because a few comedy shows without them didn't survive.

Alan believes that no matter what anyone says about "M*A*S*H," it has been fair both to the individual and the established institutions it pokes fun at. "In the beginning," he explains, "we probably sent out the signal that people were better than the institutions they serve. I don't think that's true anymore. It's more subtle now. I think what we're saying is that people aren't all bad or all good. By the same token, neither are our institutions. People make of institutions what they want them to be."

He believes that the "subtle change" came with the arrival of Harry Morgan as Colonel Potter, the new commanding officer who followed

McLean Stevenson in that role. "Potter," he explains, "is regular army, and frankly, to my surprise, we were able to develop with him a character that was both human *and* army." Potter believed in discipline, but was also experienced, compassionate, and created a father image for the assorted characters that make up "M*A*S*H." He was a guy who came from a hard-nosed military background but also had managed to maintain a sense of decency and integrity. He *was* a lift for the show.

Alan had a mixed opinion about Larry Linville's character once Larry had left the show. "There wasn't anything nice about him. He was cheap, grasping, bigoted, a hypocrite. ... I thought that was too much.... Now, a lot of people really enjoyed that character and were sorry to see him go." Then he adds, "I was, too."

A few years ago he tried to arrange a meeting between the network programmers and feminist leaders. It was one of the most frustrating experiences he ever had. "I couldn't get them [the network executives] to meet with anyone." They evaded Alan as if he came bearing the plague. They weren't interested in meeting with "any more protest groups."

"I've had some truly depressing discussions on this subject," he wearily admits, "with network people." Once, at NBC, he was at a meeting with important biggies from the peacock network. "I wanted to know why occasionally on 'Police Woman' Angie Dickinson couldn't save a guy instead of always being rescued by one. Women *do* rescue men every day—both emotionally and physically." Alan might as well have asked them to invite a black, Jewish, gay leper to dinner. Was he crazy? Would he like to see the show's ratings drop to zero? "That's what they say in private," Alan shakes his head sadly, "but in public you can bet they'd have a different answer."

At another network, where he had presented a pilot script—one he had written—a researcher suggested that his manuscript would be improved immeasurably if "I made the man less verbal." Women, he suggested, love the strong, "silent" type. Men, he told Alan, "who talk too much are looked on as being weak." Alan tires of fighting with people with that type of mentality. Wearily, he concedes the loss of at least one round in the battle for equality. "What to do? I don't know, other than to make your feelings known somehow through letters. I've given up trying to throw my weight around. I did that before. Now I find it's better and more effective if I try to take care of my own garden." He admitted that he was unhappy with the early episodes of "M*A*S*H" in which a chauvinistic point of view seemed to prevail. "I wince when I remember those segments. I fought hard to get rid of jokes about rape. I managed to get them toned down, but not totally eliminated." Needless to say, as Alan's power and prestige increased with the ratings of "M*A*S*H," things took a turn for the better.

He enjoys writing about women, but not women who are "mere decoration, or the fulfillment of male fantasies. There are real women out there in the world and I'm determined to write about them." He was incensed when the California State Senate rejected Governor Jerry Brown's appointment of controversial actress Jane Fonda to a cultural committee. Alan joined hundreds of others in full-page paid newspaper ads condemning the state senate's action. "It doesn't really matter to me," he declared, "whether Jane is on the council or not, though I think she'd probably have done a good job. I don't get inflamed about her being turned down. What I do get inflamed about is that she was turned down through a smear. She was not allowed to defend herself. It could happen to anyone and that scares me.

"I think it hit her hard, but she's strong and she'll survive." He was right about that. Jane Fonda is used to being targeted for brickbats since she took an unpopular position in the Vietnam War, and people, especially in her home state of California, have never completely forgiven her for visiting Hanoi. Alan still felt that his and the others' point was made. "There was such an immediate response by people determined that the McCarthyism of the fifties should not be repeated that the episode may turn out to have been very useful."

He strongly supports celebrities using their position and fame to influence people in what they think and do. It would be unfair, he argues, "if they couldn't. Being unable to speak your mind simply because of your celebrity would deny you your rights, and I think that's wrong." He believes that "if you have access to the media, then you have a responsibility to keep the debate on a high level and not just endorse ideas like bars of soap." He knows as well as anybody else that this premise can be a dangerous one. Some celebrities simply can't think without a director. Alan thinks. He is one of the exceptions. He knows that, too.

Like Voltaire, Alan often finds himself in violent disagreement with his contemporaries, but is in equally violent opposition to any form of censorship of free speech. When Vanessa Redgrave came under criticism from the pro-Israel elements of the country over her open support of the Palestinian's search for a homeland, Alan considered her position insensitive to Israel but defended her right to speak out. "The campaign to stop her is misguided," he said, regarding the move to prevent her starring in the television drama about a Nazi concentration camp, *Playing for Time*. "I'm furious with her insensitivity over Israel. Just about everything she stands for—outside of her artistic life—seems to me not only reprehensible but atrocious. She's calling for armed revolution; she wants to kill me and my children." He insisted that if she makes an overt step toward bringing about such a revolution, "she should be put in jail," but until she breaks the law she should be free to do as she pleases. If she should cross over the line, however, he would like "to be the one who arrests her." In spite of this feeling, he would readily act with her if they were cast together in a project. However, he adds, "I probably wouldn't talk to her over lunch."

While defending the right of radicals, Alan never loses sight of his belief in the basic morality of his country. He even took the time to write an introduction to a book by Judith Adell and Hilary Dole Klen, *A Guide to Non-Sexist Children's Books*. The object, apparently, was to endorse the feminist movement from childhood. One advertisement for the book described the contents and Alan's feelings:

Pointing out that stories for children are dreams and that such dreams are rehearsals for reality, Alda rejoices in books that "treat boys and girls as people who have the same kinds of frailties and strengths."

However, a critic felt "the emphasis is less on shared humanity between the sexes than on role reversal—that is, on strong women and frail men."

This is an important critique, not so much for the book itself, but for Alan's general attitude about women. He often states that they are not treated equally, but does he prefer a matriarchal society in which men are subservient to women? It is a fair question, and somewhere buried beneath the Alda rhetoric, the answer lies sleeping.

Whatever Alan Alda's motives or desires, everyday life goes on and "M*A*S*H" survived another season with the following statistics and figures:

Producers of the eighth season:

> John Rappaport and Jim Mulligan. Burt Metcalfe con-
> tinued as executive producer. Directors: Charles S. Dubin
> (11); Alan Alda (4); Burt Metcalfe (4); William Jurgensen
> (1); Harry Morgan (1); Mike Farrell (2). Writers: Dennis
> Koenig (6); Thad Mumford and Dan Wilcox (4); Bob
> Colleary (1); Jim Mulligan and John Rappaport (2); Ronny
> Graham (1); Sy Rosen, Thad Mumford, and Dan Wilcox
> (1); Alan Alda and Walter D. Dishell, M.D. (1); Ken
> Levine and David Isaacs (2); Dennis Koenig and Gene
> Reynolds (1); Jim Mulligan (1); John Rappaport (1); Alan
> Alda (1); Mike Farrell (1); Thad Mumford, Dan Wilcox,
> and Dennis Koenig (1).

During this eighth season, there were thirty-three female and seventy-seven male guest stars, including Robert Alda, making his second appearance in a guest role, and Alan's brother, appearing for the first time. (Not many people know that Alan is not Bob Alda's only child. From his marriage to Flora, there is a younger son, Antony, who is also an actor. He has never had the publicity accredited to his more famous brother. When Antony got married, Alan was already on his way to stardom as Hawkeye Pierce. *The New York Times* carried the marriage notice at the bottom of the marriage announcement page in three short paragraphs, the last of which said: "The bridegroom is the younger brother of Alan Alda, the actor. He is currently a student at Juilliard School and a TV actor. He recently completed 'Three Coins in the Fountain,' a pilot production for Twentieth Century-Fox.") Gary Burghoff also came back as a guest—as Radar—in three segments.

It was the last season for which statistics were available at the time of this writing, but the trends had already been fairly well established. Male guest appearances numbered 609 in 193 episodes while there were only 256 women guests. The male/female ratio was in excess of two to one. In writing or directorial situations, women were practically nonexistent. Eight women wrote segments and one woman directed.

The show was, to be fair, mostly "staff written," which means members of the show or regular writers to the series—as well as directors— were used rather than going outside. There were, of course, some exceptions to that, but few. For whatever the reason, "M*A*S*H" was practically a closed shop to outsiders, especially women.

It would be revealing if Alan would come forward and reconcile his public statements on equal opportunities for women with the record of "M*A*S*H." It is difficult to understand how anyone with his clout on "M*A*S*H" was so busy selling feminism that he overlooked the lack of it in his own series.

CHAPTER 16

A master of promotion, Alan Alda has never worked so hard at anything as he did selling the public *The Four Seasons*, the motion picture he wrote, directed, and starred in. He seems determined to outdo what has already been done. One might call him the middle-aged Warren Beatty, although he has never come close to Beatty's success as an actor, producer, director, or writer. Beatty makes films that excite and stimulate; Alda preaches until you start remembering sitting in an old country church on Sunday morning, bored to death with long-winded sermons about hellfire and damnation. Alda's films send more messages than Western Union, most of which should be marked "Addressee Unknown—Return to Sender." He moralizes at the same level as Jerry Falwell, Billy Graham, and Oral Roberts without the fire and adrenaline-hyping electrification of a good evangelist.

Nowhere has he sermonized more than with his explanations of the "message" of *The Four Seasons*, the first of a three-picture, multi-million-dollar contract between him and Universal Pictures. All three films to be written and directed by—and also star Alan Alda.

Alda's character in *The Four Seasons*, Jack Burroughs (a somewhat smart-assed New York lawyer), is similar to Alda the man. He loves the good life, as does Alda (although he keeps it good at what he calls a "moderate" level), talks to the point of being preachy and pontifical, and is also a workaholic. In *Joe Tynan* and other films, critics and others insist that Alan Alda, also like John Wayne, plays Alan Alda.

He was quick to capitalize on the parallel, however, "It's true that Jack Burroughs is closer to my own self than any other role I've ever portrayed. It's satiric of my own character, like the fact that I like to take off on verbal riffs that I find stimulating but other people either have to put up with or decide is charming in order to be my friend."

In *The Four Seasons*, his character says, "No matter what kind of crap I get from people, all I do is smile. I never give a response that's anything but rational and fair and cheerful."

Since Alda wrote the script, perhaps he was talking to himself when the Jack Weston character says to him: "There's always a little part of you that hangs back—and judges. You always want to get to the bottom of things, but only so long as you make the rules." Was Alan, in essence, telling himself to stop being so manipulative—to allow others to be less than perfect without becoming victim of his criticism? Arlene Alda occasionally tells him not to be "preachy," but she defends the qualities he instills in his films. "These," she says, "are the qualities that Alan values and he has been integrating them all his whole life."

In an interview with Carey Winfrey of *The New York Times Magazine*, while plugging *The Four Seasons*, Alan displayed no small amount of irritation over being thought of as "nice."

"I'm not too crazy about that word. I believe I'm fair. I place a high value on equity—so much so that not only do I think it is important to be fair to other people, but I am very eager to take the trouble to make sure they're fair with me."

Alda is not at all charming when angered and is the first to admit it. "I'll call a liar a liar to their face. That doesn't bother me in the least. As a matter of fact, it gives me pleasure to do that." He doesn't like being thought of as constantly being "nice."

"Nice," he declares, "is some idiot happily smiling while somebody cheats him, and that's not what I aspire to and it's not me."

In a moment of reflection, he offers an explanation for his drive. "I think one of the reasons I work so hard is to hold off despair and meaninglessness another day. Life," he says, "essentially is absurd. I think that by working you have less time to think about that."

His daughters Beatrice and Elizabeth had roles in *The Four Seasons.* "You think it's not going to be that hard," he smiles pleasantly. "Raising kids, I mean. You are sure you'll pass along to them whatever it is you have. Still, it doesn't work exactly that way. There's you, the kids, and the world they grow up in—and each is an influence." He points out that they were strict with the children—Arlene probably more so than he because she spent more time with them. The two of them joke about things, secure in the knowledge that they probably did a good job with bringing the girls up.

Arlene cites an example of the Aldas' conservatism when she notes that at sixteen their daughters' friends all had cars of their own. "I thought the girls were too young for automobiles, so I said no to that."

Then there is a bit of banter back and forth between Arlene and Alan. Alan begins to make a joke out of what she has just said. "But what about the airplane?"

"Maybe the airplane was a bit much," she laughs, "but I really think we should have sold the yacht."

"They needed the yacht for summers," Alan says as they both break up. One senses an easy-chair sense of comfort between this husband and wife, who have been married twenty-six years and know each other's habits and thoughts as well as any two people in love for so long have a right to know. Not only has Arlene given up the solitary life of homemaker and taken up her career again in music, but she brought her camera along while Alan made *The Four Seasons.* The still shots she captured became a best-selling book *On Set,* which told the story of the filming of *The Four Seasons* in pictures.

Arlene Alda is Alan's most redeeming quality. She complements his every idea and decision. She has that instinctive facility for being right in her own judgments without being judgmental. A warm, smallish woman with very dark curly hair, Arlene refuses to wear makeup. She is polite, deemed to be a great hostess, and looks you directly in the eye when she speaks to you, just as she does when someone is talking to her. You get the distinct impression that she listens and cares that you have taken the time to converse with her.

She credits their long marriage, living with a career (which is always difficult), to personal chemistry. Love is important, she says, but "we both have maintained a good sense of humor. We are constantly in each other's thoughts." For instance, they read to each other, and when reading the paper, they constantly interrupt each other to share an interesting item or thought. They are friends, too. "I can't imagine having a husband who wasn't my best friend."

What did the two of them learn as a result of experiencing *The Four Seasons* together? Alan says he doesn't know and asks the question, "What *did* we learn?"

"I don't know what you learned," she chides. "I only know what I learned. I grew just by letting go." She assures him she wasn't on location to serve as an "overly protective wife." She was president of the corporation that made the film.

Alan allowed that it was a happier time for him, just having Arlene around. "Being happily married is not that difficult," Alan explains, "as long as you know what you care about. If you have conflicts over the things you want—desiring something other than what you have— then you may find doubts."

Arlene feels that he overly simplifies it. "It's not that easy," she says. "We operate mostly based on what's happening around us. Fashion dictates, and right now, the fashion is for change." She adds that that is unfortunate. "I satisfy my needs for excitement by tasting something different, but I know the difference, I'm happy to say, between foods and people."

The Four Seasons is a contemporary film dealing with the friendships of three couples, which become so strained they almost split at the seams. Alan was delighted with the results of the film. "I think everyone has to go through these stages," he explains, "from casual to close." The spring of friendship, he says, is when you take pleasure in each other because you're apparently flawless; by summer, quirks and eccentricities start to appear; in the fall you begin to ask of and expect things of friends that you're never going to get; and by the winter you have to decide if it's all worth it or should you start from scratch.

"In a way," he says philosophically, "we're all doomed to one another ... and the doomed part is that it's almost impossible to get what we want from each other." He believes you have to learn to tolerate, to accept."

He readily admits that the part he plays in *The Four Seasons* is a satire on that part of himself he doesn't like. "That's the part I'm not proud of." Burroughs is all surface and no substance. "Seeing myself up there on the screen liberates me from having to be that person," Alan confesses.

Alan, describing himself as a realist, believes that one should make a deal with people. "Let's you and me go have fun," he says. "That way, neither one of us will have expectations that won't be fulfilled." He sounds decidedly like the irresponsible Hawkeye Pierce with that line.

San Francisco Chronicle columnist Gerald Nachman, whose column logo includes a meat cleaver, recently took a jaundiced look at Alda. With tongue in cheek, he said, 'Something must be done about the nationwide Alan Alda orgy. He's making life miserable for all us decent, well-intentioned men ... females of every kind are making fools of themselves.... He's cute but caring. His hair falls in a darling if studied rumple. When he smiles, his eyes crinkle boyishly. When he's being sincere, his eyes turn to deep pools of priestly concern. It's been reported he even eats sensibly.

It's hard not to like him, but now I even wince at his picture. Having just read a *Ms.* interview with him, seen *The Four Seasons*, and scanned a photo book shot by his wife, I'm up to my neck in Dudley Do-Right. Alda makes Gandhi look like a real hell-raiser.'

Gerald had some views on *The Four Seasons*, however, that gave him a fighting chance. He wrote,

The film is a catechism of Enlightened Attitudes on Everything, oozing Me-ism until you wish to God someone would tell Alda and his pals to go back where they came from–Passages.

... The movie isn't awful, just awfully embarrassing, told in Relationshipese; instead of one on one, it's two on two. Seeing couples being close with each other is like watching newlyweds nuzzle. Cute, but you need to be excused.

Everyone in the movie sounds like an est graduate ... it looks like a Kodak commercial.

To his credit, Nachman says, "Alda depicts the hero as a righteous prig who talks like a nudgy wife.... Only Carol Burnett as Alda's wife, casting a baleful eye on Mr. Wonderful, appears remotely real."

Richard Schickel of *Time* magazine wrote that magazine's review of *The Four Seasons*. By way of acknowledging the fledgling, he said,

The Four Seasons is Alan Alda's promising, if imperfect, directorial debut ... Alda is particularly good at examining the male sensibility ... Alda is less secure in dealing with the women. [Rita] Moreno has no role. The Sandy Dennis character is excessively loony.... Except for the confrontation scene with Alda, Carol Burnett is a bystander. ... It may be that as a writer-director, Alda is too eager to please.

... Still, American movies are rarely as alert as The Four Seasons is to the tensions implicit in friendship ... and one cannot help responding warmly to the good work of an obviously decent man.

In addition to Alda and Carol Burnett, the film starred Len Cariou, Sandy Dennis, Rita Moreno, Jack Weston, Bess Armstrong, Elizabeth Alda, Beatrice Alda, Robert Hitt, Kristi McCarthy, and Loren James (who also performed stunts). It took *The New York Times'* Janet Maslin to give the picture the push it needed and, certainly, a tremendous lift to Alan's faith in himself. Ms. Maslin concluded:

> *The Four Seasons is a fond, generous movie about characters who might have easily lent themselves to satire. Alan Alda, who wrote and directed the film and fits comfortably into its balanced cast, shapes the material almost as if he were offering a toast.*

> *...Mr. Alda sees the humor, the trouble, and the sweetness in their lives, and lets his audience see them, too.*

Aljean Harmetz reported in *The New York Times* that Mr. Alda ... has obviously brought his audience with him to the big screens. According to research by one studio ... the interest in *The Four Seasons,* a rueful comedy about a group of friends who take vacations together, is attributable almost completely to Mr. Alda and is almost entirely on the part of women.

Interestingly, the two big pictures released that week were both from Universal, and although both had comedy, they were diametrically opposed to each other. *The Four Seasons* opened in 600 theaters to a five-day gross of nearly $6 million, while Richard Pryor's *Bustin' Loose* was the big competition, grossing almost $7 million in 725 theaters for the same time period.

The Times seemed to have every critic available commenting on Alda's film. Vincent Canby was kind. "*The Four Seasons,*" he sweetly chirped, "is actually so nice that if it were one ounce nicer it would cave-in like an overloaded sponge cake. It would also cave in if it weren't played with such comic self-assurance by the stars." He finishes with, "*The Four Seasons* isn't completely convincing, but it's always attractive."

Doing interviews to promote his picture, Alan managed not to make them all duplicated copies of the original. He is a genius at saving a "never-before told" tidbit for each interviewer, which is a proper balance that most actors couldn't possibly manage. But Alda is no ordinary actor in the sense of the word. He is ambitious, powered by some unseen motive that keeps pushing him through a maze of projects that somehow always seem to get fin-

CHAPTER 17

In order to make any valid summation of Alan Alda, certain factors in his personality must be explained and examined. For instance, Alan Alda is a highly opinionated man. He tells actors how to act, directors how to direct, and writers how to write. Additionally, he has taken on the various state legislatures in his campaign to force enactment of the ERA. He has been given honorary doctorates, degrees, and awards. Like other celebrities of his ilk, he is invited to speak at a potpourri of gatherings, not so much because of his respected brilliance, but more because he is a celebrity, and celebrities draw crowds.

He dishes up advice freely. When he addressed a graduating class of doctors from Columbia University's prestigious College of Physicians, he had plenty to tell them about their profession, and these learned men sat spellbound as this accomplished silver-tongued storyteller wove his web of intrigue over them.

"I am not a doctor," he told them. "But you have asked me, and all in all I think you made a wonderful choice." He advised them if they chose to model themselves after Hawkeye Pierce, that indeed was a wise and thoughtful choice, since "he's human enough to make mistakes and yet he hates death enough to push himself past his own limits in order to save lives.

"In many ways he's the doctor patients want to have and doctors want to be. But he's not an idealization. Finding himself in a war, he's sometimes angry, sometimes cynical, sometimes a little nuts. ... If this image of that very human, very caring doctor is attractive to you ... then I'm here to cheer you on. Do it. Go for it."

Hawkeye Pierce is for fun, not for real. So, to address an assemblage of several hundred doctors and advise them to emulate this man is more comedic than the show itself. Actors have always had a tendency to take themselves too seriously. Alan Alda seems to be trying to corner the market on humility, sincerity, fatherhood, family, and brains. Again, it is dangerous when actors begin to think of themselves as experts, disastrous when anyone takes them seriously. Acting originated as a form of entertaining monarchs and royal courts. They were applauded, showered with gifts, and often revered socially—but never taken into the councils of decision making.

Alan was traveling with some rather lofty academic companions. Not only was he passing out advice to doctors, but also receiving one of the most prestigious awards in the country. Harvard University's Hasty Pudding Club selected him as their man of the year in 1979 and Meryl Streep, his costar in *The Seduction of Joe Tynan*, as woman of the year.

Scheduled to speak at commencement exercises of the graduating class of the University of California at Davis Medical School, Alan sent a telegram to the Chancellor and canceled out because of their previous rejection of Jane Fonda. He said the school had "unwittingly contributed to a climate that will create a chilling effect on the community." His loyalty to friend and cause is unquestioned.

With his duties as hovering father practically over, he is now free to turn toward other things, and he probably will, adding them to an already burgeoning schedule. His daughter Eve is now a graduate psychologist, while Beatrice and Elizabeth are drama majors and perhaps will follow their father and grandfather into "the business."

In the midwinter of 1983, "M*A*S*H" went off the air in a two-hour flame of glory with the end of the Korean War and the beginning of life ever after for Alan Alda and the cast of the 4077th Mobile Army Surgical Hospital, that mythical hospital somewhere near the front lines of a conflict that happened over thirty years ago. "M*A*S*H" on television lasted over four times the actual war. It had grown thin. The 1982 Emmy Awards, unlike previous years, gave "M*A*S*H only two statuettes: one to Alan for outstanding actor in a comedy series and one to Loretta Swit, outstanding actress in a comedy series—a far cry from the days when "M*A*S*H walked away with everything but the Price-Waterhouse representatives.

Alan certainly knew the end was near, as did the producers of the show. They were running out of plot material. How many ways can a field hospital in small quarters be presented?

Alan has tasted power. Being a controlling factor in a long-running series is tantamount to being the speaker of the state assembly or, if the star has powerful enough a personality, the Speaker of the House of Representatives. Alan has enjoyed that level of leadership. Alda should take note of power and its decline. Frank Sinatra once ruled Hollywood, as did Jack Webb. Neither maintained the control he once had. Theirs was alleged to have been a ruthless kind of reign—just as some have accused Alan Alda of perpetrating. Popularity is sustained by a top-rated series. One only needs to reach back two or three years to Farrah Fawcett or Suzanne Somers to realize how quickly stardom evaporates. Alan lucked out. He has never been considered "great" as an actor. Sugar is sweet, but too much is sickening. How long can he maintain an image of "Mr. Nice Guy"?

He has never been what one could describe as a major film star, nor have his pictures been artistically acclaimed. Commercially they have not set any records. Despite his many popularity awards, Alda still may be one of those once-a-week television freaks who cashed in on his father's fame, pushed, shoved, and clawed his way into a successful situation comedy that owes its success to skilled producers, promoters, writers, and directors (especially during the early segments of "M* A*S*H), plus a strong supporting cast that managed to add something new and interesting to the show as one after another of the originals departed. It might be added, that much of the attention that was showered on Alda came about because of his activities *away* from the "M*A*S*H" set in support of causes like the ERA and the abolition of the death penalty. Alan Alda has identified himself with the "working man" in various ways, for example, by walking a picket line (together with Loretta Swit, Mike Farrell, and Ed Asner) when the actors went out on strike.

Alan, like a clique of others who star consistently in a series, could not be equated with the average working actor who works only a few weeks (if he's lucky to be working at all) a year. The actors' strike was thought to have benefited the big stars many times over what it did for the journeyman actor. Still, the spotlights were on Alda and other millionaire superstars.

Where has Alan scored and erred?

When he made the television movie *The Glass House*, he accepted a role that was antiestablishment. The script was designed to show that criminals were unfairly treated. Their victims were not considered. In the Caryl Chessman story, *Kill Me if You Can*, his role emphasized cruel and inhuman punishment because the state of California allowed Chessman to remain on death row for twelve years while he extended his date of execution through the appeals system. Those responsible for protecting society from the criminal element felt that Chessman, whose brutal rape of one young girl put her into a mental institution, had been treated fairly—and even given preferential treatment, with little focus on the victims of his crimes.

Alda was reported to have "anguished" over the execution of Gary Gilmore by firing squad at the Utah State penitentiary, in spite of the trail of murder and cruelty left in the wake of Gilmore's homicidal rampages.

More than any other cause, Alan has espoused the ERA and "rights of women." He will probably be remembered for his zealot's drive for women's rights rather than as a superstar in one of television's longest running weekly series. It has also been the failure of ERA to pass that Alan will remember as the most disappointing event in his forty-seven years.

It seems almost presumptuous to talk about a man's "life" when he is only forty-seven years old, but we live in times when celebrities are prone to write their life story at various stages. Shelley Winters wrote what would be considered a voluminous life story in her first book and is now producing a second autobiography. So perhaps it is not so presumptuous after all to do phase one in the life of Alan Alda. Here, then, in summation, is Alan Alda the man, the actor-director-writer, the advocate of ERA and abolition of the death penalty, and as parent and family man.

Alan the man. Alan Alda is not merely one man—he is a conglomerate of people. His feelings vacillate daily, but he has the ability to bring his associates in close when he is attacked or put upon. Yet when Jackie Cooper took him to task in his own autobiography, Alan faced the cold criticism alone. He has proved, nonetheless, to be a man who remembers his friends. Rita Moreno, Carol Burnett, Jack Weston, and Mike Farrell come to mind immediately as people to whom Alda has reached out and shown the hand of true friendship.

His refusal to sign autographs is flimsy. Much of the kind of person Alda is was reflected in a 1979 interview with Thomas Thompson of *Life* magazine. Regarding autographs, Alan weakly argued, "Sure, it only takes a few seconds to sign one, but then there's another waiting ... it could be two hours out of your day." He seems to ignore an ironclad adage of show business: Without fans, there are no stars. "I like being alone ... taking care of myself," he says. Picking up the telephone in his dressing room, responding to the ring that seems to annoy him, he quickly rejects the caller: "I don't accept calls from people I don't know." He unceremoniously hangs up the receiver, with a look of annoyance at being disturbed.

Alan is a man who humbly confesses that he loves writing. "I use it as a way not to be lonely." Alda admits that he also loves a good lawsuit—"but I don't get into lawsuits unless I think I can win." He has gone after businessmen who have attempted to play him as a fool. "I sued the pants off them and won. I loved it," he says, "because I like to stick up for myself." He says that he is "aggressive, but not hostile," declaring that he is more interested in "restitution" than revenge.

"I really don't have a lot of ideas about how things should be done," he has said, expressing himself about being directed by other directors, "unless I am in charge." Until he became an official "story consultant," Alan swears he did not make many suggestions. "I would rarely make a suggestion, but now I'm franchised to make suggestions." He considers it a part of his job. He states that "there's a tradition of television stars running shows just because they've got some kind of prominence. I had plenty of prominence but didn't make suggestions until I had the title—until I was paid to do it and requested to do it. I wouldn't have presumed to do that before I had the official capacity." It would be interesting to hear the opinions of several directors about Alan's declaration about them. Why did Alan feel he was capable of being a "consultant"? Along with Gene Reynolds and Burt Metcalfe, "I was the only one in the creative end of it with continuity on the show." It was a way, he said, "of keeping the show up to what it had been."

It is also interesting to know that Alan Alda disdains awards and personal plaudits as an individual. "I wouldn't feel bad if they did away with awards and lists entirely. I don't need to be at the top of a list that keeps people out of work."

Although Alan rarely accepts an invitation to a party, if he is involved in any way with a special event, attendance is considered mandatory. An example involves his wife, Arlene. When she put together *On Set*, a picture account of Alan's film *The Four Seasons*, the then-chairman of the board of Twentieth Century-Fox, Dennis Stanfill, threw a party for Arlene Alda honoring the publication of her book. It was no coincidence that Fox released the film, which Alan—a Fox star via "M*A*S*H"—wrote and directed. It is a tribute to Alan's personal prestige and clout as a box-office attraction that the red carpet was dragged out and every creative personality under the aegis of Fox and "M*A*S*H" was commanded front and center for the affair. As a money-maker, Alan has been in a position to create his own "happenings."

Alan's adulation by his public is not unanimous. When the *Los Angeles Times* ran an article in its Calendar section about Bobby Zarem's hype to put *The Four Seasons* on the map, several readers expressed their personal opinions of the Alda hype. Kay Anderson, from Ventura, California, didn't buy the PR drivel. Of the article, she wrote that it "helped to confirm my suspicion that Alan Alda is one of the great phonies of our time." She felt that Bobby Zarem was to be admired since "it must not be easy to perpetuate the 'shy, self-effacing' image of a man who appears on the cover of every magazine on the newsstand, is on every talk show on the tube, and gets interviewed more often than the White House press secretary." The woman went even further with her brutal analysis of television's answer to the NBC peacock. She writes,

Alda is a well-publicized supporter of NOW and the Equal Rights Amendment, a self-proclaimed feminist, and frequently points to his wife's successful independent career as evidence he believes in a woman's right to her own identity and achievements. Yet in *The Four Seasons*, the one character for whom we are obviously supposed to feel dislike and contempt is the career-woman wife played by Sandy Dennis. She is a professional photographer who has wasted years taking four still lifes of vegetables, who is selfish, silly, and abandons her husband in favor of following her own contemptibly pathetic career.

There is much to be said in his favor. He has been voted in a *People* magazine poll the "person you would most like to have over at your house for dinner." In 1982, he was voted second only to President Ronald Reagan as most respected man in the world.

John Podhoretz of the *Los Angeles Herald-Examiner* said, "He has an attractive, handsome face with a prominent nose and a wry, eloquent yet colloquial way of talking. These qualities obviously please some parts of the population."

Podhoretz credits the "New Sentimentality" in which "truths are revealed to the characters every fifteen minutes or so through catharsis and love." Part of it, he contends, must have to do with Alda's style as a writer. "His lessons are pills sugar-coated by grainy photography and banter that only a worldly-wise eleven-year-old would very much appreciate."

He is an example to his audience of the perfect new American man, says Podhoretz. "He does not think of women in terms of penis envy." In fact, he continues, "Alda seems to be suffering from vagina envy."

He is what we used to call "true blue." Scout's honor to Alan is the same as an oath taken before God. Everybody knows that Alan will stand by you until the very end. He is quite human, and vulnerable, as evidenced by his loss of $145,000 (along with many other celebrities who lost more) to a phony oil scheme that was peddled around Hollywood a few seasons ago. His neighbors in Leonia have become famous with their quotes and interviews lauding Alan as a nice neighbor and credit to the community. Just an ordinary guy, they would say. "He even had us over to a barbecue—and there was no way, unless you knew of course, that anyone would pick him to be a movie star. Absolutely no way."

His peers, or many of them, in films and television praise him as a "genius," a man without faults. Mike Farrell, Carol Burnett, Rita Moreno, Loretta Swit, and Mario Thomas have all publicly acclaimed Alda as a wonderful man, a man of unequaled fairness, a man who cares, a man you can trust. Those are triple A credentials from people who have worked with him and know him well. Victor

Kemper, who directed the photography on *The Four Seasons,* sees Alan as a man of "patience and almost inevitable willingness to give people the benefit of the doubt."

Says Jack Weston, with whom he has been involved in several projects, "He brings a total innocence and a complete trust. That look on his face says, 'I really just want this to be a terrific film and I know you're going to help me.

"He hasn't lost an ounce of the joy he gets out of his work," Rita Moreno says. She should know because their relationship goes back to the days of Alan's "walking the boards" in the road company of *The Owl and the Pussycat.*

When Carol Burnett was asked if she thought Alan wasn't taking on too many hats and should perhaps stick to acting, she responded in patented Carol Burnett fashion. "I'd say, if you've got it, flaunt it. I think Alan's going to pave the way for other actors to show what they can do."

"M*A*S*H and Alan Alda. Robert Altman created the motion picture "M*A*S*H. He and Alan Alda have both expressed their antiwar positions. Alan speaks of "M*A*S*H," the television series, as discouraging war. Altman believes the television series should never have been made in the first place. "I have absolutely no feeling about how good it is," he shrugs somewhat aloofly. "I just wish it hadn't been done. It is wrong to make a TV series out of a closed piece of work. To continue it is to diminish the positive effect of the film as an antiwar statement. The continuation of the series is a continuation of the apathy about war. It becomes the same thing as watching the Vietnam War on television."

When the show celebrated its two hundredth episode, those who departed as regulars were not invited back to enjoy the soiree, which included champagne and a large cake. Trying to keep the party lively, executive producer Burt Metcalfe said, "All of those who left the show still get along great with the regulars they started out with." He admitted the relationship was no longer as close as it had once been. A year later, when the tenth season was completed and the film in the can, there was another party. Colin Dangaard wrote from Hollywood, "It's more like a wake than a party. People are gathered here to praise a show, but they've also come to bury it." Everyone knew that the end was upon them, still nobody really wanted to voice such an opinion. Nonetheless, it was Burt Metcalfe who expressed the realities of a series running out of gas. "How many times can you say war is hell, the food is rotten, and why don't we all go home?"

Alan Alda, Dangaard reported, "was looking more like he'd lost his dog than celebrating a ten-year birthday party for an idea that made him a household name."

"M*A*S*H" was pretty much "group written" by people associated on a regular basis with the show. Often the writing sessions resembled a round-table discussion at the "funny farm." Producer John Rappaport sees that as part of the series' success. "What you must be willing to do in those meetings," he told Steve Gelman of *TV Guide*, "is make a fool of yourself; the essence of good group writing is 'never be afraid to say something stupid.'"

Alan has said, "The very concept of this show brings out the best in you; to be funny and let the pain come through." When it was announced that "M*A*S*H" would go into permanent hiatus, Metcalfe said, "You want to go while you still have a little punch left. You don't want to be like an old boxer who just fights himself into oblivion."

Alan and the ERA. Next to "M*A*S*H," Alan's pitch for women's rights has made him more famous than acting, writing, or directing combined. One columnist prayed, "Please, God, don't ever let Alan Alda get divorced." The women's movement, she said, would survive Billie Jean King's confessions of lesbianism, but it was doubtful it could overcome the decline and fall of "the perfect new man."

Because of Alan, a few other men have come forward to state the case for women. Not many have been as fervent as Alda. Women have trusted him with their torch and would rather not hear anything bad about him. He is their knight in shining armor. He found it difficult to accept when he discovered that a male friend had been cheating on his wife. "Temporarily," he somberly whispered, "I found it hard to relate to him."

It is easy, some men have pointed out, for Alan to be a feminist. He has his own security and a traditional wife who stayed home and brought up the children. After all, didn't she give up her career so that he could have one? Times change. He and Arlene were married nearly three decades ago when it was more fashionable for women to stay home in the traditional manner of Old World Jewish and Italian families. He has repeated time and time again, since he took up the cudgel to defend women, that he regrets having deprived Arlene of her equal right to a career. "I hope I have a chance to make it up to her," he says. Arlene smiles and assures everyone that she wouldn't change a single day of their life together, that she has enjoyed bringing up their daughters to adulthood. Alan might not have had all those years of uninterrupted marriage had Arlene been the type to insist that Alan practice then what he preaches today. It is easy to stand up for women when your own wife is purring softly in the background and not making "deprived woman" noises. The Phyllis Schafleys of the world might point to Alan's marriage as the classic reason for women not to support the ERA. The long, successful, traditional marriage of Alan and Arlene Alda may have hurt the cause that Alan has so tenaciously fought to make a reality.

Alan's case for ERA has been submitted with the same fervor and dedication with which Clarence Darrow, the famous criminal attorney, might have defended a client caught with his hands dipped in a victim's blood. "In the Constitution," he argues, "there's no clear signal to our courts that inequality under the law with regard to sex is inherently wrong... you can say that women are not in the Constitution."

He doesn't see ERA as a panacea for the complaints of women in America. "It only deals with law," he points out. It does not force employers to treat women equally in the work force—to open up new avenues of employment that are on a par with those of men. Employers, he argues, "must be educated to realize that all of the mediocre men that are being hired in industry might as well be mediocre women—or women who are twice as good at the job but are being ignored in the marketplace through the hiring of less capable men."

Alan has spent much of his ERA time trying to convince *men* that women wouldn't necessarily be drafted into combat. He sees women who would be drafted replacing men in less physically demanding jobs in order to release men for the more physically demanding jobs including combat. This might pose a question of reverse discrimination. If women have equal rights, then shouldn't they also have equal obligations to fight side by side in the trenches with men. Alan calls that the big fear that the anti-ERA advocates use to persuade the mostly male legislators to vote against the amendment.

Alan has never hesitated to bring his family of women—a wife and three daughters—into the fray. Speaking to the Hollywood Women's Press Club, where he received an award as star of the year in 1979, he said, "The only thing wrong with ERA is that we don't have it yet. Erma Bombeck says that the twenty-four words in the ERA are the most misunderstood since the slogan 'one size fits all.'"

"Why," he asked, "am I so concerned about ERA in other states when I live in New Jersey? I have daughters. When they leave home, I don't want them to have to shop around the country to find a place to live." He emphasized the unequal pay that women were receiving in same jobs men held. He cited an item from *U.S. News and World Report*, which stated that the average high school male dropout earns more than the average woman college graduate. In his own field, he said, "Only fifteen percent of Screen Actors Guild members earn a living wage and of the other [eighty-five percent] there are five times as many women as men unemployed." He urged his own industry to put more women to work behind the camera. "M*A*S*H," meanwhile, was taking almost as long to recognize women behind the camera as the various state legislatures were in recognizing their constitutional rights.

Warming up an audience, Alan once said in jest, "You hear those old bromides about how if ERA is passed all sorts of bad things will happen, like using the same bathrooms. Well, so far every state that okayed ERA still has His and Her signs out and you're not likely to find a woman in a men's washroom unless she's fixing the plumbing!"

Alda has pooh-poohed the "woman on a pedestal" cliché that is supposed to be part of the chauvinistic male animal's values. "'Honey,'" he states, "is an inappropriate way to start a conversation unless you are a bear talking to your lunch."

Gloria Steinem, editor of Ms. magazine and one of the most effective feminists in the country, thinks so highly of Alda's contributions that she once MC'd a tribute to him, which drew two thousand of his fans. When a man at the function approached him and asked why men should be willing to give up their "privileged position" in the male/ female scheme of things, Alan suppressed a bristle as he responded, "Not give up, but *share*. Power is not in limited supply, like gold. It is more like manure: If you spread it around, things will grow better." It was an evening at which Alan raised several thousand dollars for the Ms. Foundation.

It is men, however, that Alan has concentrated on as the missing element in the feminist drive for equality. He never made a more impassioned plea to his fellowmen than in a speech before the New York chapter of the National Women's Political Caucus on February 22, 1979. He singled out men who were reluctant to openly support the ERA drive:

"I want to speak mostly to men ... I want to set a fire under you.... But if you men out there are in favor of the Equal Rights Amendment because of the women in your lives, then you've missed the boat. You have to be for it because it means something to you personally.... We and our companions and our daughters and our mothers and our sisters all are being systematically deprived. They're calling for our help. That's why I'm asking you men to get involved in the fight for equal rights ... not because you will be helping women, but because you will be helping yourself. I don't want you to be profeminist. I want you to be a feminist... I want you to be a *fighter* for ERA ... I'm asking for your *passion!*"

Male passions did not rise to Alan's expectations and the ERA died during the summer of 1982 when the last possible states being lobbied by Alan and his friends, Oklahoma and Illinois, turned thumbs down on the proposed amendment to the Constitution. It was a devastating defeat for Alan, since he had put so much of his time and energy into the effort and was so certain (as were the many pro-ERA groups) that his voice would have an impact on other men in legislative bodies. Nobody will ever be able to say that Alan Alda did not give it everything he had. It simply was not enough.

Alan's other causes. Alan rarely attacks individuals espousing his various causes. He did, however, make an exception in the case of Congressman Robert K. Dornan. After listening to Dornan deliver an address in Houston several years ago, he decided that he was for most of what Dornan was against. The following excerpts from a guest editorial that Alan wrote for *The Village Voice*, although expressing a negative view of Congressman Dornan, reveal an extensive list of personal beliefs of the very private Alan Alda:

> *I watched Congressman Dornan whip his listeners into a frenzy of fear and hatred using every tool he could—including religious fervor—to move his audience to reject equality and freedom of choice for one-half of the human race.*
>
> *I knew in that moment that this was a man who is not serving the interests of the people of the United States.*
>
> *I wished at that moment that I could do something about the way he was trying to destroy what we were fighting so hard to achieve.... That's why I want to alert you to*

*Congressman Robert Dornan and how he threatens some
of our most important rights in this country.*

He denounced the Supreme Court for allowing even limited abortions, saying "God will not be mocked." He then announced he was introducing a constitutional amendment giving a fetus the "right to life" from the moment of conception.

He served as "Congressional adviser" to the Christian Voice, a far-right fundamentalist group whose projected three-million-dollar budget for the 1980 election is aimed at "eliminating abortion, sex and violence on television, homosexual rights," promoting total opposition to the Salt II Treaty and immoral U.S. policy in Rhodesia and Taiwan, where our Christian allies are being thrown to the wolves.

Dornan's support of environmental issues is so bad that the League of Conservation Voters rated him only 7 on a 100-point scale: one of the worst records in the House.

He opposes gun control, opposes the ERA, opposes abortion under all circumstances, opposes the Panama Canal Treaty, opposes SALT.

'He has attacked what he calls "extreme-right-wing" groups who will, if their "plan" is allowed to succeed, "restrict abortion rights for the poor, for military wives and daughters of soldiers, for Peace Corps volunteers and working women covered by certain health insurance policies." He opposes the calling of a constitutional convention because "once that convention opens, it could be a field day for the political right wing ... the entire Constitution of the United States would be thrown open to change. The Bill of Rights, separation of church and state, and freedom of speech could all suffer grave—even irreparable—harm. They want to impose on all of us their values, their morality, and *their* notion of what is right. They must be stopped."

What Alda seems to be saying is that his "group" wishes to make sure that another "group" is headed off at the pass, while his ethics and standards should be the ones that prevail. So, the private Alan Alda believes women have the right to have abortions. He advocates abolition of the death penalty, gun control, the Panama Canal Treaty, SALT (Strategic Arms Limitation Treaty), as well as sex and violence on television—if his editorial to *The Village Voice* represents his true feelings.

Alda has always played down being a political person, but rarely has an actor exposed himself so much to public issues.

Alan Alda the actor. Alan has won innumerable awards for his acting, writing, and directing—based on even more nominations by his peers. In 1979, Man Watchers, Inc., rated Alan number six in its ten all-time television watchables. In the television book of lists, 1981 edition, Bob Michaelson, in his list of the six hardest-to-photograph, most-uncooperative TV stars, ranked Alan number six in that list behind Miss Piggy (without makeup). Still, as recently as April 1982, the secret Q list (better known as TVQ) gave Alda its highest rating for a male with a score in the survey of 52. As an actor, however, he cannot claim that as his personal popularity input, because it was more "M*A*S*H" than Alda, evidenced by the fact that after Robert Guillaume ("*Benson*") with a 41, came three more actors: Harry Morgan, 40; Mike Farrell, 39; and Jamie Farr, 38.

Alan made his future evident as early as 1968 when the *Motion Picture Herald* made note that Alda was "becoming a man for all theater. Not just the stage, but theater in the broadest sense—actor, singer, writer, director." He is an indefatigable worker with more projects going at one time than most men can handle in a year or two. He has never come close to what he considers his potential as a creative artist.

As an artist, the one thing he has had to deal with that he feels had been disconcerting is fame. "You can possibly get drunk on fame," he grins. "I found that the impression it makes on you lasts for a little while. I mean that you're singled out as something special. Then, you understand that the fact is you still do your work as well as you can and you still have to live your life." Still, he added an appreciative tag line. "It's like having too many hundred-dollar bills on the floor. You bend over so much, your back begins to hurt. It's too much of a good thing. You can't buy a pair of socks without making a personal appearance."

Many fans, he says, are sensitive to your situation, understanding that they may be intruding on your privacy or imposing on your time. There are others, however, who "treat the acting celebrity as material to manhandle," he groans. "They don't realize that I'm a person. 'Look at him,' they say. 'Talk to him.'"

He has made a dozen movies, only two or three of which are remembered to any great degree even in the motion-picture industry. Still, he made money on them and feels that he honed his craft—even with the "dogs," which he admits quite readily were just that.

"Ideally," he explains, "I want to act with material that means something to me. Fame is the price you have to pay just to be in something you really want. If I had a choice between being rich or famous, I wouldn't ask for famous." Most actors, he suggests, are neither rich nor famous. "Nor," he adds, "are they in what they want." He believes in inspiration, but only of the personal variety. "Without that," he declares, "it doesn't matter how many other facets are involved in one's craftsmanship.

"I never wanted fame," he pointedly states. "I value my privacy, but only the famous are awarded the parts I personally want to play." He says that he accepts fame for that reason and that reason only. "I don't want my life played out in print as if it were a comic strip.

"I am not the same kind of actor that my father was, nor am I allowed to be myself as much as he was." The truth in that statement lies in the fact that in Robert Alda's day a star was supposed to "act like a star." The senior Alda's comment about that was, "I was Tiffany's, but they kept insisting on putting me in Woolworth's window." He laughs. "At Warner Brothers, that ruined my career. I ended up making Spaghetti sword-and-sandals pictures in Rome." When the studio system fell and the day of the moguls ended, actors began to take control of their own lives. Alan has been a part of that "declaration of independence," not only by actors, but by others in the creative film industry. He hasn't had to endure the humility and embarrassment of his father and other great actors who were merchandised like salami on a billboard. Alan hires expensive public relations people (like Bobby Zarem) to package and present him in the manner he desires to be seen. His father depended (through no choice of his own) on the studio to take care of such matters. It is small wonder Louis B. Mayer called actors "my children."

Alan has taken the best of his father's time and incorporated it into his own creative life. "My father and I have strong connections," he says with genuine feeling and emotion. "I love my father."

He has never aspired to being thought of as "the new John Wayne." That appealed to him about as much as the right-wing philosophies espoused by .Wayne. "I want to be the ultimate creator." (Some of his creations have barely made it to the network scanning boards. Such series as "We'll Get By" and "Hickey vs. Anybody," which starred buddy Jack Weston, were barely noticed. Still, it was part of the long tedious process toward perfecting a craft that never seems totally perfect.)

How does he feel about the position he has tirelessly sought for so many years? "I hate being on all the time. It's too much trouble and there isn't enough time in the day to do the important work I must do and still talk to several hundred people, too. I don't like to be looked at as if there isn't anyone at home inside my face."

He hasn't yet satisfied himself as an actor, writer, director, or producer. He feels that he has made some satisfying films with messages that embrace "humanness" and "life in the everyday family," but that one great epic statement is yet to be made.

Alan Alda the family man and friend. Alan has impeccable recall when it comes to people with whom he has been involved no matter how many years may have passed. His childhood girl friend Antoinette Dell'Olio (now Toni Lopopolo) reveals her experience with Alan's good memory. "Several years ago," she recalls, "I moved to New York. My sister, Anselma, went to a party there and ran into Alan. When she introduced herself, he remembered the family name. "Do you know Antoinette Dell'Olio? She's the daughter of Rose and Gerry Dell'Olio."

My sister laughed, "Of course. She's my sister. I remember you once took us to see *Frankenstein* when we were all kids in California."

Alan remembered and they renewed their acquaintance. Anselma gave Alan their phone number and he called Toni. On the telephone they caught up with all the events of their years since they were sweethearts. "He expressed great sorrow that my marriage hadn't worked out after three children. I was touched by his sincerity and concern."

Later, Toni and her three children joined Alan, Arlene, and their three children for a get-together at the Alda home in Leonia. "At our first get-together after so many years—my marriage and children, his marriage, children, and career—Alan met us in tennis togs as if we dropped in like neighbors whenever we pleased. He seemed to take real interest in my children; interested in what they had to say and what they thought. I was impressed by that.

"Arlene, in the kitchen chopping onions, was the most totally unpretentious lady I'd ever met. She couldn't have cared less that her husband and I had shared each other's first crush. She was warm and open. She and Alan appeared to be very loving toward one another and he was obviously a loving father with his girls—supportive in language—touching, hugging. And he brought flowers home to his wife. I thought to myself, after all those years to still do that. Women appreciate such a kindness from their men."

Out of that reunion in New York came an invite to a showing of Arlene's flora photography, called *"The Sensuous Leaf."*

"Bob Alda was there with his second wife. I went up to him and said, 'I'm Rose and Gerry's daughter,'" That was the beginning of a book called *99 Ways to Cook Pasta*, by Bob and Flora, which was published by Macmillan and edited, of course, by Toni, who was then an editor there. "The book," Toni explains, "was a family affair. Bob and Flora wrote it, Alan wrote the preface, and Arlene did the cover."

With some clarity of hindsight, Alan now says, "I don't think I tried to isolate my family from the show business world I've worked in. We merely decided not to give up our home and friends because I happened to work in another town." Most writers seem to blink when Alan makes statements of that nature now that his daughters are on their own and his wife is finally an independent woman.

However he has handled his family, they have been to a large degree the beneficiaries of the $5 million plus a year he is reputed now to earn. "I'm not sure that is the correct figure," Alan says with an infectious smile. After this brief lapse into humor, he waxes serious. "My whole life has become a process of doing a little bit better by my conscience each year."

Although there has been some criticism about Arlene's background role in their marriage, he isn't worrying much about the critics. His marriage, he believes, is sound. "There was a time ... when we were very dependent on one another. Learning to be independent together and still being able to enjoy each other was, I think, the biggest change from the early days of our marriage to the present."

He has also grown to appreciate the independence of his children, although when one of his daughters brought home a plaque she had made at school, he confesses that "I had to bite my tongue." The plaque read: "A woman is happiest in the kitchen." Perhaps she was merely emulating what she had seen in her own home, for Arlene spent all the girls' growing-up years in the kitchen, several hours every day.

As a husband Alan argues through his work and his life for fidelity to the family unit. "Also to myself," he adds. "I find it harmful that many people think men and women can only come together for the purposes of sex. I had to work against all of that sort of thing.

That whole patriarchal syndrome." In order to make that point on a personal level, he says, "I was on the phone with my family three and four times a day when we were apart. I'd fly out and be with them every weekend." He discovered how shallow and lonely is the man whose entire life is devoted to working, at the expense of family. The reality came to him, he says, when he was working twenty hours a day on the now-defunct television series "*We'll Get By*".

"How ironic," he thought, "that I'm writing a show about a family while I'm not being part of my own!"

Although he contends that he did not shelter his family, as far back as 1974 in an interview, he said, "Smalltown living helps me avoid much of what happens to you in California. I don't speak the language they talk out there. The TV thing can be tough on the kids ... even here [in Leonia] a teacher will occasionally hurt one of my daughters by referring not to her abilities, but to [one of] her parent's."

Someone asked him why he insisted on living in the East when all of his work was in Los Angeles. "Oh, I'm sure there are a lot of actors still living in New York. I mean, who's driving the cabs?"

He doesn't like Hollywood houses. Those places, he says, "are made to drive past at thirty miles an hour. There's a Spanish hacienda next to a Tudor house." They are both phony, he says.

"And California is a terrible place to raise your children." Since nothing is grown organically, he adds, "the kids' brains are fried in the sun."

Alan's own children attended private schools, but they all agree that being the offspring of a famous father has presented no special problems. Alan and Arlene often shopped at the local supermarket and took part in school functions just as other parents in Leonia. Familiarity, they felt, did not breed contempt. On the contrary, it caused the local citizens to look on the Aldas as just another family in town.

Their mother and father often disagreed on discipline for the girls and they took advantage, at times, of Alan's permissiveness. Elizabeth admits that "we used to put the touch on him for money because he was gone for long periods." She quickly adds, "We don't do that anymore." As he gets older, Alan confesses that he has often had a tendency to "preach." He has even admitted to being "less patient with my own sermons."

Alan doesn't just fall into friendships. He has learned to be cautious. He has learned to discern who wants to be his friend and who wants to be the friend of a celebrity. "There are ways I can tell if they're getting cozy with the celebrity," he says, explaining, "they give off signals and I ask myself why I would be valuable to them. Is it to have me show up to impress their friends? Am I someone they need to help them in business? There are other gauges, too. If people think of themselves and me as two different members of the caste system, we can never be friends." One person touching the edge of fame, he says, is not the basis of friendship.

Even in the entertainment business, he avoids any close relationship with those who "see themselves as lower" than him. He tries not to create an impression, he says, that will cause others to think of him as "above them." After explaining to one friend what he expected in friendship, he noticed the fellow looking dejected. "I don't think I measure up to your expectations," he said. That might well have been a line Jack Weston would have used in a dialogue with Alan during a scene in *The Four Seasons*.

"I used to be a Catholic," Alan told *Ms.* magazine. He left the Church, he says, "because I object to conversion by concussion. If you don't agree with what they teach, you get clobbered over the head until you do. All that does is change the shape of the head."

He doesn't like the way the Church handles its house, but admits if anyone tried to change the way he runs his own they would be out. In friends, he says, "I enjoy exchanging household hints on how to get through life."

His marriage is based on friendship. Sex, he says, doesn't break up marriages. A man can fall in love with someone besides his wife, Alan argues, but if he continues to consider his mate's feelings, friendship will see the marriage through. Sex in the marriage bed, he contends, is the same as it is anyplace else. "We are all the same in bed," he contends.

"I am not a sober person," Alan says, but he admits that he often "sounds sober." He considers himself a person who is playful and enjoys a good time with the best of them, but he has great difficulty separating his life into segments of joy and gloom because of the world around him—even when he is on a "high," he is painfully aware of the societal litter about him—the breakdown of the family, nuclear annihilation over humanity's head, and the uncertain future for children. "It is difficult to be playful or happy in the face of inequality," he has said.

"There are still terrible injustices and inequalities," he says, but he knows now that going off in all directions will not solve the problems that irritate him. "I simply don't have the energy anymore to try to change everything— this year."

He hopes his children will suffer less injustice as women because of his efforts. When his daughter Eve graduated from college, he gave the commencement address. I believe he expressed a lot of who Alan Alda is when he said, "Adulthood has come upon you and you're not all that sure you're ready for it. I think that sometimes I'm not ready for adulthood either—yours *or* mine."

If Alan is not a man who is committed to any one religion, he presents a person with deep religious convictions. Addressing the Entertainment Industries Division of the National Conference of Christians and Jews, where he was awarded their eighteenth annual Humanitarian Award in 1981, he told the crowded assemblage of industry and civic leaders who had paid $175 a plate to honor him, "My wife is Jewish, and I was raised a Catholic. Our whole marriage has been a conference of Christians and Jews." His future mother-in-law had been horribly persecuted, along with her family in Russia, by the Christian Cossacks. "Now a Christian wanted to marry her daughter. I don't know what she felt. I know what I felt from her. I felt ... warmth. She loved me openly and freely. ... I feel very grateful for the acceptance I received from her, for her letting me come into her life."

Universal Pictures president, Ned Tanen, applauded Alan at that gathering as a person who "really personifies so much of what America can be about."

The evening was capped off with a tribute from his former costar and friend, Mario Thomas. "He is an actor who acts the parts he believes, a director with a lifetime p.o.v. [point of view], a writer who's aware of himself and others around him." Injecting some humor she added, "Anyone who has driven a cab in New York and is still able to be a humanitarian deserves an award. If Alan Alda is the sex symbol of the eighties, there's hope for this country."

People magazine's third annual popularity poll in 1980, comprised of 58 percent women at a median age of 31.1, went all out for Alan Alda. He was the favorite male for three years running, predicted to be the best choice in "celebrity to next enter politics," and was once again voted the celebrity most desired as a home dinner guest. Interestingly, tied in second place as potential political hopefuls were three liberal fellow actors: Ed Asner, Robert Redford, and Jane Fonda.

During that same year, he was one of four *male* entertainers rated top television money-makers. His companions were Carroll O'Connor, Michael Landon, and Larry Hagman—with Alan, of course, grossing the largest figure at $5,625,000.

As a family man, Alan has had to deal with great variances: A mother-in-law who was a refugee from tyranny and persecution, a father who was a star, a mother who was idolized by a husband who placed her on a pedestal and then pulled the pedestal out from under her when he left her.

As blithely as Alan speaks of family harmony, there has not always been harmony. Rumors have persisted that Flora (Antony Alda's mother) feels that too much is made of Alan and not enough of her son with Bob Alda. Once, when Antony wanted to become involved with one of Alan's projects—a film—his father discouraged Antony from making the effort. "Wait until he asks you," he advised. Antony, also an actor, did not appear with Alan until 1980, when the two Alda boys, along with their father, did a segment of "M*A*S*H" together. The boys have never been close. Alan attributes that to the difference in age and the distance between them as Antony grew up. Antony does not discuss his feelings about Alan. He is even more a guardian of his private life than Alan. It is almost, in the Alda family, decreed that Alan be the official spokesman for everyone. On a few rare occasions, Bob Alda has violated that tradition.

Wherever Bob Alda appears, he is relegated to second billing to his eldest son, who may be thousands of miles away. Bob handles questions deftly, expressing genuine pride and feeling for his eldest son. "I don't mind being known as Alan's father," he says with fatherly resignation. "My dear," he reminds one motherly-looking woman, "I have *always* been Alan's father." His advice to *both* sons about acting, he says, was the same. "If you think you have the stamina and guts to be an actor, by all means, I'm ready and willing to help. I *did* open doors for them, but warned them that they better have talent, otherwise they would be shown out the back door."

The Alda men have common links besides blood. "We all are married and we all love to cook," Bob boasts. "They learned to cook from me. I spent a lot of time in the kitchen when they were growing up and they were both anxious to learn."

Of all the many people who have analyzed Alan Alda and furnished their particular expertise to help round out the complete man, the most interesting came from a handwriting expert, who saw him in a totally different perspective. His signature, the expert revealed, marked him as a "pleasure-seeker who can resist anything except temptation ... an earthly man with great capacity for the enjoyment of sensual pleasures ... will try most anything once ... you know that a constant internal battle is being waged.... He is forever fighting a lack of self-discipline by superimposing an outward veneer of control ... a man of many talents with a built-in knack for survival... good intellect, a fine sense of humor, and the ability to laugh at himself."

A number of years ago *Esquire* magazine featured Alan on its cover along with other then-current television personalities, under the headline take a good look at: THESE PEOPLE. THEY'LL BE WASHED UP IN TWO YEARS.

That error stands tall beside the *Chicago Tribune*'s famous 1948 headline, DEWEY WINS. The following day Harry S Truman was still president of the United States. Alan Alda is still king of his television domain—although "M*A*S*H" is now history.

ACKNOWLEDGMENTS

This was a most difficult undertaking and without the kindness and cooperation of many contributors of information it might never have happened. Therefore, I'd like to thank everyone who was a part of this book in that respect: Joan Brown Alda; Flora Alda; Jane Barba; Antoinette (Toni) Lopopolo; Paul Blane; Nancy Bacon; Dr. Terry Robinson; Peter and Lynda Ford; Diana Markes; Jet Fore; Leo Guild; Larry Smith of *Parade* magazine; Viveca Lindfors; Robert Zarem; Barbara Perrin; Hank Grant of the *Hollywood Reporter*; Dick Lochte (*Los Angeles Times* and *TV Guide*)', Mel Pogue—Casting Call; the editors of *Reader's Digest*;Cynthia Crossen, managing editor of *The Village Voice*; the managing editor of the *New York Sunday News*; Robert C. Smith—*TV Guide*; Howard Kissell—*Women's Wear Daily*; the Academy of Motion Picture Arts and Sciences Research Library; the Research Library—University of California at Riverside; David Alexander—*Season Ticket* magazine; the editors of *People* magazine; the editors of *The New York Times Magazine*; Carey Winfrey, Ms. magazine; *Redbook*magazine; the various editors of the *Los Angeles Times*, *Los Angeles Herald-Examiner*, *San Francisco Chronicle*, *Chicago Tribune*, *Washington Post*, and *Los Angeles Daily News*; Joseph N. Bell of *Good Housekeeping*; *Playgirl* magazine; Susan Edmiston, *Ladies' Home Journal*; Cynthia Heimel; Gerald Nachman; Gloria Steinem; Morton Moss; Paul Ehrmann (*Horizon* magazine); Peter Borsari, *Motion Picture*

Herald; Cecil Smith; James Bacon, *Emmy* magazine; John Podhoretz; Thomas Thompson *(Life* magazine); Sheilah Graham; Roderick Mann; Brock Yates, *U.S. News & World Report*; William A. Henry III, *Vogue*magazine; Gary Deeb; Elizabeth Kaye; Kathleen Hendrix; Pat Colander; Joyce Haber; *Film Facts*; Stephen Farber; Kay Gardella; James Nathan; Norma Lee Browning; Joanne Stang; *Ebony* magazine; *Seventeen*; *Facts on File*; Robert Parish *(Hollywood Players—The Forties)*; Dan Seymour; Esther Carr—editorial rights and permissions manager of *Reader's Digest*; H. Richard Hornberger, M.D.-P.A. (author of M*A*S*H).

Excerpts have been taken from "Alan Alda: Madcap Doctor from 'M*A*S*H,'" George Vecsey, *Reader's Digest* (August 1979); "It Pays Me an Extra Gall Bladder a Week," Neil Hickey, *TV Guide* (March 24, 1973); "He Falls Down a Lot," Dick Lochte, *TV Guide* (February 24, 1973); "C*L*A*S*H," Bill Davidson, *TV Guide* (January 24, 1976); "Being a Star Is a Nuisance," Dwight Whitney, *TV Guide* (June 4, 1977); "Rule No. 1: Never Be Afraid to Say Something Stupid," Steve Gelman, TV *Guide* (April 24, 1981); "The Interplay's the Thing," David Johnston, *7V Guide* (January 5, 1980); "It's—Uh, a Real Drag," Dwight Whitney, *TVGuide* (September 27, 1975); "Sometimes Mike Farrell Is So Noble ... ," John M. Wilson, *TV Guide* (March 17, 1979); "The Wonderful Wizard of Bucks," A1 Stump, *7V Guide* (July 10, 1976); "Burghoff Is for the Birds," A1 Stump, *TV Guide* (August 10, 1974); "She's What a Woman Should Be," Edwin Kiester, Jr., *TV Guide* (February 9, 1974); "Auggghhh!" Kathleen McCoy, *7V Guide* (January 30, 1971).

I would like to give a special thanks to Jackie Cooper for his generosity in permitting me to quote so extensively from his autobiography, *Please Don't Shoot My Dog* (coauthored with Dick Kleiner), published by William Morrow Co., Inc., 1981.

Also, an extra-special thanks to fellow author Doug McClelland who, more than anyone else, continued to send me clippings, photographs, and leads to sources of information about Alan Alda. Doug is one of those rare writers who believes in other writers.

Nothing I could say would truly reveal the debt I owe Kenneth Norris of Toronto, Canada, who travels several thousand miles to be sure that the book jacket photo of me is just the right one, takes hundreds of shots to assure that, and promotes my works as if they were his own. I thank you most sincerely, my friend.